THE BAFUT BEAGLES

Also by Gerald M. Durrell

THE OVERLOADED ARK

GALAGOS

The
BAFUT BEAGLES

by Gerald M. Durrell

Illustrated by Ralph Thompson

New York · 1954

THE VIKING PRESS

Copyright 1954 by Gerald M. Durrell
Published by The Viking Press in October 1954

Several excerpts of this book
appeared in *Harper's Magazine*.

Library of Congress catalog card number: 54-9600

Printed in the U.S.A. by Vail-Ballou Press, Inc.

For
KENNETH SMITH
In memory of Fons,
false teeth, and
flying mice

CONTENTS

ILLUSTRATIONS

THE BAFUT BEAGLES

IN WHICH WE DONE COME

The Cross River picks its way down from the great mountains of the Cameroons until it runs sprawling and glittering into the great bowl of forest land around Mamfe. After being all froth, waterfalls, and eager chattering in the mountains, it settles down when it reaches this forest and runs sedately in its rocky bed. The gently moving waters create ribs of pure white sand across its width and wash the mud away from the tree roots, so that they look as though they stand at the edge of the water on a tangled writhing mass of octopuslike legs. It moves along majestically, its brown waters full of hippo and crocodile, and the warm air above it filled with hawking swallows, blue and orange and white.

Just above Mamfe the river increases its pace slightly, squeezing itself between two high rocky cliffs, cliffs that are worn smooth with the passing of the waters and wear a tattered antimacassar of undergrowth that hangs down from the forest above; emerging from the gorge, it swirls out into a vast egg-shaped basin. A little farther along, through an identical gorge, another river empties itself into this same basin, and the waters meet and mix in a skein of tiny currents, whirlpools, and ripples, and then continue onwards as one waterway, leaving, as a result of their marriage, a huge glittering hummock of white sand in the centre of the river, sand pockmarked with the footprints of hippo and patterned with chains of bird tracks. Near this island of sand the forest on the bank gives way to the small grassfield that surrounds the village of Mamfe, and it was here, on the edge of the forest, above the smooth brown river, that we chose to have our base camp.

It took two days of cutting and levelling to get the campsite ready, and on the third day Smith and I stood at the edge of the grassfield watching while thirty sweating, shouting Africans hauled and pulled at what appeared to be the vast, brown, wrinkled carcass of a whale that lay on the freshly turned red earth. Gradually, as this sea of canvas was pulled and pushed, it rose into the air, swelling like an unhealthy-looking puffball. Suddenly it seemed to spread out and turned itself into a marquee of impressive dimensions. When it had thus revealed its identity, there came a full-throated roar, a mixture of astonishment, amazement, and delight, from the crowd of villagers who had come to watch our camp in the building.

Once the marquee was ready to house us, it took another week of hard work before we were ready to start collecting. Cages had to be erected, ponds dug, various chiefs from nearby villages interviewed and told of the animals we required, food supplies laid in, and a hundred and one other things. When the camp was functioning smoothly we felt we could start collecting in earnest. We had decided that Smith, my companion, should stay in Mamfe and keep the base camp going, gleaning what forest fauna he could with the help of the local inhabitants, while I was to travel farther inland to the mountains, where the forest gave place to the great grasslands. In this mountain world, with its strange vegetation and cooler climate, fauna completely different from that of the steamy forest region was to be found.

I was not certain which part of the grasslands would be the best for me to operate in, and so I went to the District Officer for advice. I explained my dilemma, and he produced a map of the mountains. Together we pored over it. Suddenly he dabbed his forefinger down and glanced at me.

"What about Bafut?" he asked.

"Is that a good place? What are the people like?"

"There is only one person you have to worry about in Bafut, and that's the Fon," he said. "Get him on your side, and the people will help you all they can."

"Is he the chief?"

"He's the sort of Nero of this region," said the D.O., marking a great circle on the map with his finger, "and what he says goes. He's the most delightful old rogue, and the quickest and surest way to his heart is to prove to him that you can carry your liquor. He's got a wonderful villa there, which he built in case he had any European visitors, and I'm sure if you wrote to him he would let you stay there. It's worth a visit, is Bafut, even if you don't stay."

"Well, I'll drop him a note and see what he says."

"See that your communication is—er—well lubricated," said the D.O.

"I'll go down to the store and get a bottle of lubrication at once," I assured him.

So, that afternoon, a messenger went off to the mountains, carrying my note and a bottle of gin. Four days later he returned, bearing a letter from the Fon, a masterly document that encouraged me tremendously.

Fon's Office Bafut
Bafut Bemenda Division
5th March, 1949

My good friend,

Yours of 3rd March, 1949, came in hand with all contents well marked out.

Yes, I accept your arrival to Bafut in course of two month stay about your animals and too, I shall be overjoyed to let you be in possession of a house in my compound if you will do well in arrangement of rentages.

Yours codially,
Fon of Bafut

I made arrangements to leave for Bafut at once.

1.   TOADS AND DANCING MONKEYS

The majority of West African lorries are not in what one would call the first flush of youth, and I had learned by bitter experience not to expect anything very spectacular of them. But the lorry that arrived to take me up to the mountains exceeded anything that I had seen before: it tottered on the border of senile decay. It stood there on buckled wheels, wheezing and gasping with exhaustion at having to climb up the gentle slope to the camp, and I consigned myself and my loads to it with a certain amount of trepidation. The driver, who was a cheerful fellow, pointed out that he would require my assistance with two very necessary operations: first, I had to keep the handbrake pressed down when travelling downhill,

for unless it was thus held, almost level with the floor, it sullenly
refused to function. Second, I had to keep a stern eye on the
clutch, a wilful piece of mechanism that seized every chance
to leap out of its socket with a noise reminiscent of a strangling
leopard. As it was obvious that not even a West African lorry
driver could be successful in driving while crouched under the
dashboard in a prenatal position, I had to take over control of
these instruments if I valued my life. So, while I ducked at
intervals to put on the brake, amid the aromatic smell of burning rubber, our noble equipage jerked its way towards the
mountains at a steady twenty miles per hour. Sometimes, when
a downward slope favoured it, it threw caution to the winds
and careered along in madcap fashion at twenty-five.

For the first thirty miles the red-earth road wound its way
through the lowland forest, the giant trees standing in solid
ranks alongside and their branches entwined in an archway of
leaves above us. Flocks of hornbills flapped across the road,
honking like the ghosts of ancient taxis, and on the banks,
draped decoratively in the patches of sunlight, the agama
lizards lay, blushing into sunset colouring with excitement and
nodding their heads furiously. Slowly and almost imperceptibly
the road started to climb upwards, looping its way in languid
curves round the forested hills. In the back of the lorry the
boys lifted up their voices in song:

> Home again, home again,
> When shall I see ma home?
> When shall I see ma mammy?
> I'll never forget ma home . . .

The driver hummed the refrain softly to himself, glancing at
me to see if I would object. To his surprise, I joined in, and

while the lorry rolled onwards, trailing a swirling tail of red dust behind it, the boys in the back maintained the chorus, and the driver and I harmonized and sang complicated bits. The driver also played a staccato accompaniment on the horn.

Breaks in the forest became more frequent the higher we climbed, and presently a new type of undergrowth made its appearance: massive tree ferns standing in conspiratorial groups at the roadside on their thick, squat, hairy trunks, the fronds of leaves sprouting from the tops like delicate green fountains. These ferns were the guardians of a new world, for suddenly, as though the hills had shrugged themselves free of a cloak, the forest disappeared. It lay behind us in the valley, a thick pelt of green undulating away into the heat-shimmering distance, while above us the hillside rose majestically, covered by a coat of rippling, waist-high grass bleached golden by the sun.

The lorry crept higher and higher, the engine gasping and shuddering with this unaccustomed activity. I began to think that we should have to push the wretched creature up the last two or three hundred feet, but we made it, and the lorry crept on to the brow of the hill, trembling with fatigue, spouting steam from the radiator like a dying whale. We crawled to a standstill and the driver switched off the engine.

"We go wait small time, engine get hot," he explained, pointing at the forequarters of the lorry, which were by now completely invisible under a cloud of steam. Thankfully I descended from the red-hot interior of the cab and strolled down to where the road dipped into the next valley. From this vantage point I could see the country we had travelled through and the country we were about to enter.

Behind lay the vast forest, looking from this distance as

tight and impenetrable as green lamb's wool; only on the
hilltops was there any apparent break in the smooth surface of
those millions of leaves, for against the sky the trees were sil-
houetted in a tattered fringe. Ahead of us lay a world so different, so dissimilar, that it seemed incredible that the two should
be found side by side. There was no gradual merging: behind
lay the forest of huge trees, each clad in its robe of polished,
glittering leaves; ahead, to the farthermost dim blue horizon, lay
range after range of hills, merging and folding into one another
like great frozen waves, tilting their faces to the sun, covered
from valley to crest with a rippling fur of golden-green grass
that paled or darkened as the wind curved and smoothed it.
Behind us the forest was decked out in vivid greens and scarlets,
harsh, intense colours; before us, in this strange mountain
world of grass, the colours were soft and delicate, fawns, pale
greens, warm browns, and golds. The hills covered with this
pastel-tinted grass could have been an English scene: the down-
land country of the south on a larger scale. The illusion was
spoiled, however, by the sun, which shone fiercely and steadily
in a completely un-English manner.

From there the road resembled a switchback, and we rattled
and squeaked our way down into valleys and coughed and
grunted our way up the steep hillsides. We had paused on one
hilltop to let the engine cool again, and in the valley ahead I
noticed a village, looking at that distance like an irregular
patch of black toadstools against the green. When the engine
was switched off the silence descended like a blanket. All we
could hear was the soft hiss of the grass moved by the wind,
and, from the village far below us, came the barking of a dog
and the crowing of a cockerel, the sounds tiny and remote

but clear as a bell. Through my field glasses I could see that there was some activity going on in the village. Crowds of people milled round the huts, and I could see the flash of machetes and spears and the occasional glint of a gaudy sarong.

"Na whatee dat palaver for dat place?" I asked the driver.

He peered down the hill, screwing up his eyes, and then turned to me, grinning delightedly. "Na market, sah," he explained, and then said hopefully, "Masa want to stop for dat place?"

"You tink sometime we go find beef for sale dere?"

"Yes, sah!"

"For true?"

"For true, sah!"

"You lie, bushman," I said in mock anger. "You want to stop for dis place so you go find corn beer, no be so?"

"Eh! Na so, sah," admitted the driver, smiling, "but sometimes Masa go find beef there also."

"All right, we go stop small time."

"Yes, sah," said the driver and sent the lorry hurtling down the slope towards the village.

The big huts, with their conical thatched roofs, were grouped neatly round a small square shaded by groups of young eucalyptus trees. In this square was the market. In the patchwork of light and shadow under the slim trees the traders had spread their wares on the ground, each on his own little patch, and around them thronged the villagers in a gesticulating, chattering, arguing wedge. The wares offered for sale were astonishing in their variety and, sometimes, in their incongruity. There were fresh-water catfish dried by wood smoke and spitted on short sticks. These are unpleasant-looking fish when alive, but when dried and shrivelled and blackened by the smoking they look like fiendish little juju dolls twisted into strange contortions by a revolting dance. There were bales of cloth, some of it the brightly coloured prints so beloved of the African, imported from England; more tasteful was the locally woven cloth, thick and soft. Among the patches of cloth was an odd assortment of eggs, chickens in bamboo baskets, green peppers, cabbages, potatoes, sugar cane, gory hunks of meat, giant cane rats neatly gutted and hung on strings, earthenware pots and cane baskets, eroco wood chairs, needles, gunpowder, corn beer, gin traps, mangoes, pawpaws, enemas, lemons, native shoes, lovely raffia-work bags, nails, flints, carbide and cascara, spades and leopard skins, plimsolls, trilbies, calabashes full of palm wine, and old kerosene tins full of palm and groundnut oil.

The inhabitants of the market were as varied and as curious as the wares offered for sale: there were Hausa men clad in brilliant white robes and little white skullcaps; local chieftains in multicoloured robes and richly embroidered caps with tassels; Pagans from distant mountain villages, wearing nothing but a scrap of dirty leather round the loins, their teeth filed to points, their faces tattooed. For them this represented a teeming metropolis, and the market was perhaps the high spot of the year's amusements. They argued fiercely, waving their arms, pushing one another, their dark eyes shining with delight over such things as cocoa yams or cane rats; or they stood in little groups gazing with hopeless longing at the toppling piles of multicoloured cloth, milling round from one vantage point to another, in order to get the best views of these unobtainable luxuries.

My staff and the lorry driver disappeared into this pungent, swirling crowd like ants into a treacle tin, and I was left to wander round by myself. After a time I decided to try to take some photographs of the Pagan tribesmen, and I set up the camera and started to focus it. Immediately pandemonium broke loose; the tribesmen with one accord dropped their goods and chattels and fled for the nearest shelter, screaming wildly. Rather bewildered by this, for the average African is generally only too pleased to have his photograph taken, I turned to a Hausa standing close by and asked him what was the matter. The explanation was interesting: apparently the Pagans knew what a camera was, that it produced pictures of the people it was pointed at. But they were firmly convinced that with each photograph taken the photographer gained a small portion of his subject's soul, and if he took many photographs he would gain complete control over the person in question. This is a good example of witchcraft brought up to date; in the old days if you obtained some of your victim's hair or toenails you had great power over him; nowadays, if you get a photograph it apparently acts just as well. In spite of the reluctance on the part of my subjects I managed to get a few shots of them, by the simple method of standing sideways to them, looking in the opposite direction, and taking the photographs from under my arm.

It was not long, however, before I discovered something that drove all thoughts of photography and witchcraft out of my head. In one of the dark little stalls that lined the square I caught a flash of reddish fur, and, moving over to investigate, I found the most delightful monkey on the end of a long string, squatting in the dust and uttering penetrating "prroup" noises.

PATAS MONKEY

She had light ginger-coloured fur, a white shirtfront, and
a mournful black face, and the strange noises she was making
sounded like a cross between a bird cry and the friendly greet-
ings of a cat. She sat and watched me very intently for a few
seconds, and then she got up and started to dance. First she
rose on her hind legs and jumped up and down vigorously,
holding her long arms wide apart as though she were going to
clasp me to her bosom. Then she got down on all fours and
started to bounce like a ball, all four feet leaving the ground,
her jumps getting higher and higher the more excited she be-

came. Then she stopped and took a short rest before starting on the next part of the dance, which consisted of standing on all fours, keeping her hindquarters quite still, and flinging her forequarters from side to side like a pendulum. Having demonstrated the outline, she then showed me what could be done by a really experienced dancing monkey. She twirled and leaped and bounced until I felt quite dizzy. This wild dervish dance was irresistible, and I felt that I simply had to buy her. I paid her owner twice what she was worth and carried her off triumphantly. I bought her a bunch of bananas at one of the stalls, and she was so overcome by my generosity that she repaid me by wetting all down the front of my shirt.

I rounded up the staff and the driver, all breathing corn beer, and we climbed into the lorry and continued our journey. The monkey sat on my knee, stuffing her mouth with banana and uttering little cries of excitement and pleasure as she watched the scenery out of the window. In view of her accomplishment I decided to call her Pavlova, and Pavlova the patas monkey she became forthwith.

We drove on for some hours, and by the time we were nearing our destination the valleys were washed with deep purple shadows and the sun was sinking leisurely into a thousand scarlet and green feathers of cloud behind the highest range of western hills. We knew when we reached Bafut, for there the road ended. On our left lay an enormous dusty courtyard surrounded by a high red brick wall. Inside was a great assembly of circular huts, with high thatched roofs, clustered round a small, neat villa. But all these structures were dominated and dwarfed by an edifice that looked like an old-fashioned beehive magnified a million times. It was a huge circular hut, with a

massive domed roof of thatch, black and mysterious with age.
On the opposite side of the road the ground rose steeply, and
a wide flight of some seventy steps curved upwards to a large
villa, shoebox shaped, its upper and lower stories completely
surrounded by wide verandas, the pillars of which were profusely hung with bougainvillia and other creepers. This, I
realized, was to be my home for the next few months.

As I stiffly got out of the lorry an arched doorway in the
far wall of the great courtyard opened, and a small procession
made its way across to where I stood. It was a group of men,
most of them elderly, clad in flowing multicoloured robes that
swished as they moved; on their heads they wore little skullcaps thickly embroidered in a riot of coloured wools. In the
midst of this group walked a tall, slim individual with a lively,
humorous face. He was dressed in a plain white robe, and his
skullcap was innocent of decoration, yet you at once singled
him out as the only one of any importance in the little caval-
cade, so regal was his manner. He was the Fon of Bafut, ruler
of the great grassland kingdom we had been travelling through
and its immense population of black subjects. He was incredibly wealthy, and he ruled his kingdom, I knew, with intelli-
gent, if slightly despotic, cunning. He stopped in front of me,
smiling gently, and extended an extremely large, slender hand.

"Welcome," he said.

It was not until later that I learned he could speak pidgin
English as well as any of his subjects, but for some reason he
was shy of his accomplishment, so we talked through an interpreter, who, bent deferentially, translated my speech of
welcome through his cupped hands. The Fon listened politely

and then waved one huge hand at the villa on top of the slope above me.

"Foine!" he said, grinning.

After shaking hands again he walked back across the court-yard with his councillors and disappeared through the arched doorway, leaving me to get installed in his "foine" house.

Some two hours later, when I had bathed and eaten, a messenger arrived and informed me that the Fon would like to visit me for a chat if I had sufficiently "calmed" myself after my journey. I sent back a reply to the effect that I was quite calmed and would be delighted to receive a visit from the Fon. I got out the whisky and awaited his coming. Presently he arrived, accompanied by his small retinue, and we sat on the veranda in the lamplight and talked. I drank his health in whisky and water, and he drank mine in neat whisky. We talked at first through an interpreter, but as the level of the whisky fell the Fon started to speak pidgin English.

For two hours I was fully occupied in explaining my mission in his country. I brought out books and photographs of the animals I wanted. I drew them on bits of paper and made noises like them when all else failed, and all the time the Fon's glass was being replenished with frightening regularity. He said he thought I should be able to get most of the animals I had shown him, and he promised that, the next day, he would send some good hunters to work for me. But, he went on, the best thing for him to do was to spread the word among his people so that they would all try to catch "beef" for me. The best opportunity for this, he explained, would be in about ten days' time, when a certain ceremony was to be held. His subjects, on an appointed day, gathered large quantities of dry grass from the hills and valleys and brought it into Bafut so that the Fon could rethatch the roof of the great juju house, and the roofs of his innumerable wives' houses. When the grass had been brought in he provided food and drink for a feast. Many hundreds of people assembled from all over the surrounding countryside would be at the ceremony, and it would be an ideal opportunity, the Fon said, to make a speech explaining what I wanted to his people.

I agreed heartily, thanked him profusely, and refilled his empty glass. The level in the bottle fell lower and lower, until it was innocent of even the most reluctant drops of liquid. The Fon rose majestically to his feet, stifled a hiccup, and held out a hand.

"I go!" he proclaimed, waving a hand in the vague direction of his small villa.

"I'm sorry too much," I said politely. "You like I go walk for road with you?"

"Yes, my friend," he said, beaming. "Na foine!"

I called for a member of the staff, who came running at the double, carrying a hurricane lantern. He preceded us as we walked down the veranda towards the steps. The Fon was still clasping my hand in his, while with the other one he gestured at the veranda, the rooms, and the moonlit garden some thirty feet below, muttering "foine, foine" to himself in a self-satisfied way. When we reached the top of the long flight of steps he paused and stared at me pensively for a moment, then pointed downwards with one long arm.

"Sheventy-foif step," he informed me.

"Very fine," I agreed, nodding.

"We go count um," said the Fon, delighted at the idea. He draped a long arm round my shoulders, leaned heavily upon me, and we descended to the road below, counting loudly.

As he could not remember the English for any number higher than six we got somewhat confused halfway down, and, on reaching the bottom, we found that according to the Fon's reckoning there were three steps missing.

"Sheventy-two?" he asked himself. "No, na sheventy-foif. Which side dey done go?"

He glared fiercely at his cringing retinue, who were waiting in the road, as though he suspected them of having secreted the missing steps under their robes. Hastily I suggested that we count them again. We climbed up to the veranda, counting wildly, and then, to make quite sure, we counted them all the way down again. The Fon kept counting up to six and then starting again, and I could see that unless something was done we should spend all night searching for the missing steps; so, when we reached the top, and again when we got to the bottom, I said, "Seventy-five!" in loud triumphant tones and beamed at my companion. He was a bit reluctant to accept my reckoning at first, but I assured him that I had won innumerable prizes for mental arithmetic in my youth and that my total was the correct one. He clasped me to his chest, clutched my hand and wrung it, muttering, "Foine, foine, my friend," and then wended his way across the courtyard to his own residence, leaving me to crawl up the seventy-five steps to bed.

The next day, in between coping with a headache brought on by my session with the Fon, I was kept busy building cages for the flood of specimens I hoped would soon be rolling in. At noon four tall, impressive-looking young men turned up, clad in their brightest sarongs and carrying ancient flintlocks. These fearsome weapons were incredibly old, and their barrels were pitted and eroded with rust holes, as though each gun had suffered an acute attack of smallpox. I got them to stack these weapons outside the gate before they came in and talked to me. They were the hunters the Fon had sent, and for half an hour I showed them pictures of animals and explained how much I would pay for the various creatures. Then I told them to go away and spend the afternoon hunting, and to return in the evening with anything they caught. If they caught nothing they were to come early the following morning. I distributed cigarettes, and they wandered off down the road, talking earnestly to one another and pointing their guns in all directions with great abandon.

That evening one of the four young men turned up with a small basket. He squatted down and gazed at me sorrowfully while he explained that he and his companions had not had very good luck with their hunting. They had been a considerable distance, he said, but had found none of the animals I had shown them. However, they had got *something*.

He leaned forward and put the basket at my feet. "I no savvay if Masa want dis kind of beef," he said.

I removed the lid of the basket and peered inside. I thought that it might contain a squirrel, or possibly a rat, but there sat a pair of large beautiful toads.

"Masa like dis kind of beef?" asked the hunter, watching my face anxiously.

"Yes, I like um too much," I said, and he grinned. I paid him the required sum of money, dashed him some cigarettes,

BROW-LEAF TOADS

and he went off promising to return the following morning with his companions.

When he had gone I turned my attention to the toads. They were each about the circumference of a saucer, with enormous liquid eyes and short fat legs that seemed to have difficulty supporting the heavy bodies. Their coloration was amazing: their backs were a rich cream colour, sprinkled with minute black vermiculations; the sides of the heads and bodies were a deep red, a cross between mahogany and wine; and their bellies were a vivid buttercup yellow.

I have always liked toads, for I have found them quiet well-behaved creatures with a charm of their own; they have not the wildly excitable and rather oafish character of the frog, nor his gulping, moist appearance. But, until coming into contact with these two, I had always imagined that all toads were pretty much the same, and that, having met one, you had met them all as far as personality was concerned, though they might differ much in colour and appearance. I very soon discovered that these two amphibians had personalities so striking they might almost have been mammals.

These creatures are called brow-leaf toads because the curious cream-coloured marking on the back is, in shape and colour, exactly like a withered leaf. Crouching down on the floor of the forest, the toad merges into its background perfectly—hence its English title. Its scientific title is even more apt: it is *Bufo superciliarus*. The latter word is happily chosen, for the brow-leaf, on first acquaintance, gives the impression of being overwhelmingly supercilious. Above its large eyes the skin is hitched up into two little points, so that the creature has its eyebrows raised at the world in a markedly sardonic manner. The immensely wide mouth adds to this impression of aristocratic conceit by drooping gently at the corners, thus giving the toad a faintly sneering expression that can be achieved by only one other animal that I know of, the camel. Add to this the slow, swaggering walk, and the fact that the creature squats down every two or three steps and gazes at you with a sort of pitying disdain, and you begin to feel that the person who christened it *Bufo superciliarus* was exercising grim restraint.

My two brow-leafs squatted side by side on a bed of fresh grass in the bottom of the basket and gazed up at me with expressions of withering scorn. I tipped the basket onto its side, and they waddled out onto the floor with all the indignation and dignity of a couple of Lord Mayors who had been accidentally locked in a public lavatory. They walked about three feet across the floor and then, apparently exhausted by this effort, they squatted down, gulping gently. They surveyed me very fixedly for some ten minutes with what appeared to be ever-increasing disgust before one of them wandered away and eventually crouched down by the leg of the table, evidently under the mistaken impression that it was the trunk of a tree. The other one continued to stare at me and, after much mature reflection, summed up its opinion of my worth by being sick, bringing up the semidigested corpses of a grasshopper and two moths. It gave me a pained and reproachful look and joined its friend under the table.

As I had no suitable cage ready the brow-leafs spent the first few days locked in my bedroom, wandering slowly and meditatively about the floor, or squatting in a trancelike state under my bed, and affording me untold amusement by their actions. I found, after a few hours' aquaintance with my plump roommates, that I had sadly misjudged them, for they were not the arrogant, conceited creatures they pretended to be. They were really shy and easily embarrassed, completely lacking in self-confidence.

I was making notes on their coloration, while the toads squatted on the floor at my feet, looking as though they were composing their own entries for Burke's Peerage. Wanting to examine their rear regions more closely, I bent down and picked up one of them between finger and thumb, holding it under the armpits, so that it dangled in the air in a most undignified manner. The toad uttered a loud indignant belch and kicked out with fat hind legs, but my grip was too strong, and it just had to dangle there until I finished my examination. When I put the toad back on the ground next to its companion it was altogether different. Gone was the aristocratic expression: it was a deflated, humble amphibian. It crouched down, blinking its great eyes nervously, while a sad and timid expression spread over its face. It looked almost as if it were going to cry. The transformation was so sudden and complete that it was astonishing, and I felt absurdly guilty at having been the cause of its ignominy. To even things up a bit I picked up the other toad and let it dangle for a while, and it too lost its self-confidence and became timid and embarrassed when I replaced it on the floor. They sat there looking so dejected and miserable that it was ludicrous, and my unmannerly laughter proved too much for their sensitive natures, for they waddled rapidly away and hid under the table for the next half-hour. But once I had learned their secret I could deflate them at will when they became too haughty: all I had to do was to rap them gently on the nose with my finger, and they would crouch down guiltily, looking as though they were about to blush, and gaze at me with pleading eyes.

I built a nice large cage for my brow-leafs, and they settled down in it quite happily. However, to keep them healthy, I allowed them to have a walk in the garden every day. When the collection increased there was so much work to be done that I could not stand around patiently while my two blue-blooded aristocrats took the air, and I had to cut down on their walks, much to their annoyance. Then, one day, I found a guardian in whose hands I could safely leave them while I got on with my work. This was none other than Pavlova the patas monkey.

Pavlova was extremely tame and gentle, and she took an intense interest in everything that went on around her. The first time I put the brow-leafs out for a walk near her she was quite captivated and stood up on her hind legs, craning her neck, to get a better view as they walked sedately across the compound. Ten minutes later, when I went back to see how the toads were getting on, I found that they had both wandered close to the spot where Pavlova was tied. She was squatting between them, stroking them gently with her hands and uttering loud purring cries indicative of astonishment and pleasure. The toads had the most ridiculously self-satisfied expressions on their faces, and they were sitting there unmoving, apparently flattered and soothed by her caresses.

Every day after that I would put the toads out near where Pavlova was tied, and she would watch them wandering about. She would give occasional cries of amazement at the sight of them, or else stroke them gently until they lay there in a semi-hypnotized condition. If ever they wandered too far away and were in danger of disappearing into the thick undergrowth at the edge of the compound, Pavlova would get very excited and with shrill screams let me know that her charges were escaping. I would hurry down and bring them back to her. One day she called me, but I did not hear her, and when I went down some time later she was dancing hysterically at the end of her string, screaming furiously. The brow-leafs were nowhere to be seen. I undid the monkey's leash, and she led me towards the thick bushes at the edge of the compound. Within a very short space of time she had found both the runaways and had fallen on them with cries of joy.

Pavlova really got terribly fond of these fat toads, and it was quite touching to see how eagerly she greeted them in the morning, and how worried she got when they wandered too

PAVLOVA AND THE TOADS

far away. She found it very difficult to understand why the toads were not clad in fur, as another monkey would be. She would touch their smooth skins with her fingers, endeavouring to part the nonexistent fur, a worried expression on her little black face; occasionally she would bend down and lick their backs in a thoughtful sort of way. Eventually she ceased to worry over their baldness, and she treated them with the same gentleness and affection she would have displayed to offspring of her own.

The toads, in their own curious way, seemed to get quite fond of her as well, though she sometimes upset their dignity, which annoyed them. One morning, just after I had given them both a bath that they thoroughly enjoyed, they got various bits of stick and dirt stuck to their wet bellies, walking across the compound. This worried Pavlova, for she liked her protégés to be clean and neat. I found her sitting in the sunshine, her feet resting on the back of one brow-leaf as though it were a footstool, while the other one dangled in the most undignified fashion from her hand. As the toad slowly revolved in midair Pavlova solemnly picked off all the bits of rubbish, talking all the time in a series of squeaks and thrills. When she had finished she put it on the ground, where it sat looking very crestfallen, while its partner was hoisted up into the air and forced to undergo the same indignity. The poor brow-leafs had no chance of being superior and pompous when Pavlova was around.

2.   THE BAFUT BEAGLES

In order to hunt for the various members of the Bafut fauna
I employed, besides the four hunters the Fon had supplied, a
pack of six thin, ungainly mongrels, who, their owners assured
me, were the finest hunting dogs in West Africa. I called this
untidy ensemble of men and dogs the Bafut Beagles. Although
the hunters did not understand the meaning of the title they
grew extremely proud of it, and on one occasion I heard a
hunter, when arguing with a member of the local population,
proclaim in shrill and indignant tones, "You no go shout me like
dat, ma friend! You no savvay dat I be Bafut Beagle?"

Our hunting method was as follows: we would walk out to
some remote hillside or valley and choose a thick patch of

grass and bushes. At a suitable point we would spread our nets in a half-moon shape; then, with the dogs, we would walk through the undergrowth, driving whatever creatures we found into the nets. Each dog wore a little wooden bell round its neck, so that when the pack disappeared into the long grass we could still keep track of its whereabouts by the loud clonking noise from the ornaments. The advantage of this method of hunting was that I was on the spot to handle the creatures from the very moment of capture, and they could be hastily taken back to Bafut and placed in decent cages with the minimum of delay. We transported our captures in bags with special air holes, ringed with brass, let into the sides; for the bigger and tougher creatures the bags were of canvas or hessian, and for the more delicate beasts they were made out of soft cloth. Once in the darkness of the bag the captives generally ceased to struggle and lay quite quietly until we got them home. The most frightening part of the whole process from the animals' point of view was the disentangling from the net, but after a bit of practice we got this part of the job down to a fine art, and an animal could be caught, removed from the nets, and placed in a bag within the space of two minutes.

The first day that I went out with the Bafut Beagles the hunters turned up so heavily armed one would have thought we were going out to hunt a lion. Apart from the usual machetes, they were carrying spears and flintlocks. As I did not fancy receiving a backside full of rusty nails and gravel I insisted, amid much lamentation, that the guns be left behind. The hunters were horrified at my decision.

"Masa," said one of them plaintively, "if we go meet bad beef how we go kill um if we go lef' our gun for dis place?"

"If we go meet bad beef we go catch um, no kill um," I said firmly.

"Eh! Masa go catch bad beef?"

"Na so, my friend. If you fear, you no go come, you hear?"

"Masa, I no de fear," he said indignantly, "but if we go meet bad beef and it go kill Masa, de Fon get angry too much."

"Hush your mouth, my friend," I said, producing a shotgun, "I go take my own gun. Den if beef go kill me it no be your palaver, you hear?"

"I hear, sah," said the hunter.

It was very early morning, and the sun had not yet risen above the encircling mountain ranges. The sky was a very delicate shade of rose pink, trimmed here and there with a lacing of white cloud. The valleys and hills were still blurred and obscured with mist, and the long golden grass at the roadside was bent and heavy with dew. The hunters walked ahead in single file, the pack of dogs scampering in and out of the undergrowth, their bells making a pleasant clonking as they ran. Presently we turned off the road and followed a narrow twisting pathway that led over the hills. Here the mist was thicker but low-lying. You could not see the lower half of your body, and you got the eerie impression that you were wading waist-deep in a smooth, gently undulating lake of foam. The long grass, moist with dew, squeaked across my shoes, and all around me under the surface of this opaque mist lake tiny frogs were sharing an amphibian joke with one another in a series of explosive chuckles. Soon the sun rose like a frosted orange above the distant fringe of hills, and as its heat grew stronger the mist started to rise from the ground and coil up to the sky, until it seemed as though we were walking

through a forest of pale white trees that twisted and bent, broke
and re-formed with amoebic skill, as they stretched and spiralled
their way upwards.

It took us two hours to reach our destination, a deep, wide
valley lying between two ridges of hills, curving slightly like
a bow. Along the bottom a tiny stream made its way between
black rocks and golden grass, glinting in the sun like a fine
skein of spun glass. The undergrowth in the valley was thick
and tangled, shaded here and there by small clumps of shrubs
and bushes.

We made our way down into the valley and spread about
a hundred yards of nets right across it. The hunters took the
dogs and went to the head of the valley, while I waited near
the nets. For half an hour there was silence as they moved
slowly towards the net, a silence broken only by the faint
sounds of the dogs' bells and an occasional shrill expletive
from the hunters when one of them trod on a thorn. I was
just beginning to think we had drawn a blank when the
hunters started a great uproar and the dogs began barking
furiously. They were still some distance away, hidden from
my view by a small clump of trees.

"Na whatee?" I shouted above the noise.

"Na beef for dis place, Masa," came the answer.

I waited patiently, and presently a panting hunter burst
through the trees.

"Masa, you go give me dis small catch net," he said, pointing
at the smaller nets neatly piled beside the bags.

"Na what kind of beef you done find?"

"Na squirrel, sah. 'E done run for up stick."

I picked up a thick canvas bag and followed him through

the undergrowth until we reached a small clump of trees.
Here the hunters were grouped, all chattering and arguing as
to the best way of catching the quarry, while the dogs leaped
and barked round the trunk of a small tree.

"Which side dis beef?" I asked.

" 'E dere dere for up, Masa."

"Na fine beef dis, Masa."

"We go catch um one time, Masa."

I stepped to the base of the tree and peered up into the
foliage; there, perched on a branch some twenty feet above
us, was a large, handsome squirrel, brindled grey in colour,
with a white stripe along his ribs and orange paws. His tail
was long and not bushy, banded faintly with grey and black.
He squatted on the branch, occasionally flipping his tail at us
and crying "chuck! chuck!" testily, as though he were more
irritated than anything else. He watched us with a malevolent
eye while we set up the nets in a circle, about ten feet away
from the base of the tree. Then we tied up the dogs, and the
smallest of the hunters was detailed to climb up and drive the
squirrel down. This part of the operation was the hunters'
idea; I felt that to try and outmanoeuvre a squirrel in a tree
would be impossible, but the hunters insisted that once someone
climbed up, the squirrel would come down to the ground. As
it turned out they were quite right; no sooner had the hunter
reached the upper branches on one side of the tree than the
squirrel shot down the trunk on the other side. With incredible
cunning he dashed at the one portion of the net that had a
tear in it, struggled through the hole, and galloped off through
the grass, the hunters and myself in hot pursuit, all of us shouting instructions to one another which were completely disre-

SIDE-STRIPED SQUIRREL

garded. We rounded a clump of bushes to see the squirrel scrambling up the trunk of another small tree.

Once again we spread the nets, and once again the hunter climbed up. This time, however, our quarry was more cunning, for he saw that we were guarding the hole in the net through which he had escaped last time. He ran down the tree trunk to the ground, gathered himself into a bunch, and jumped. He sailed through the air and cleared the top of the net by about half an inch. The hunter nearest to him made a wild grab but missed, and the squirrel galloped off, chuck-chucking indignantly to himself. This time he decided on new evasive tactics, and instead of climbing up a tree he dived into a hole at the base of one of them. We surrounded the tree with nets, and then started to poke long slender sticks down into the network of tunnel in which he was hiding. This, however, had no effect whatsoever, except to make him chuck a bit faster, so we gave it up.

Our next attempt was more successful: we stuffed a handful of smouldering grass into the largest hole, and as the pungent smoke was swept through the various tunnels we could hear the squirrel coughing and sneezing angrily. At last he could bear it no more and dashed out of one of the holes, diving head first into the nets. But even then he had not finished causing trouble, for he bit me and two of the hunters while we were disentangling him, and bit a third hunter while he was being forced into a canvas bag. I hung the bag on the branches of a small bush, and we all sat down to have a much-needed smoke. The squirrel peered at us through the brass-ringed air holes and chattered ferociously, daring us to open the bag and face him.

The side-striped ground squirrels are common enough in the grasslands of West Africa, but I was pleased to have caught this one, as he was the first live specimen I had obtained. As their name implies, these squirrels are almost completely terrestrial in their habits, and so it rather surprised me to see the one we had caught taking refuge up in the trees. I discovered later that all the grassland squirrels (most of which *are* terrestrial) made straight for the trees when pursued and chose holes in the ground or hollow logs only as a last resort.

When we had bound up our wounds and congratulated one another on our first capture, we moved the big net farther down the valley to an area where the grass was thick and tangled and almost six feet tall. This was a good place for a special kind of beef, the hunters informed me, though with understandable caution they refused to specify what kind. We set up the net, I placed myself at a suitable point halfway along its length and inside the curve, so that I could disentangle anything that was caught, and the hunters took the dogs and made their way about a quarter of a mile up the valley. They gave a prolonged yodel to let me know they had started to beat through the long grass, and then silence descended. All I could hear was the whir and tick of innumerable grasshoppers and locusts, and the faint sounds of the dogs' bells.

Half an hour passed, and nothing happened. I was hemmed in by tall rustling grass so thickly interwoven that it was impossible to see through for more than a couple of feet. The tiny clearing in which I was sitting shimmered with heat, and I began to feel extremely thirsty. Looking round, I noticed something that I had forgotten: a thermos flask of tea that my thoughtful cook had stuck into one of the collecting bags.

Thankfully I got it out, and, squatting down at the edge of the long grass, poured myself a cup. As I was drinking I noticed the mouth of a dark tunnel in the wall of grass opposite me. It was obviously some creatures' private pathway through the forest of grass stalks, and I decided to investigate it after I finished my drink.

I had just poured out my second cup of tea when a terrific uproar broke out to my right, startlingly near at hand; the hunters were uttering shrill yelps to encourage the dogs, and the dogs were barking furiously. I was wondering what it was all about when I head a rustling noise in the grass and moved closer to the tunnel to try to see what was causing it. Quite suddenly the grass parted and a large dark brown shape hurled itself out of the hole and ran straight into me. I was at a distinct disadvantage: to begin with, I was not expecting the attack, and second, I was squatting on my heels, clasping a thermos flask in one hand and a cup of tea in the other. The animal—to my startled eyes it seemed to be twice the size of a beaver—landed amidships, and I went flat on my back, with the creature on my stomach and the thermos flask pouring a stream of scalding tea into my lap. Both the creature and I seemed equally astonished, and we both gave vent to shrill squeals of fright that were almost identical. With hands full I could do nothing more than make a wild grab with my arms, but the animal bounced off me like a rubber ball and scuttled off through the grass. A portion of the net started to jerk and quiver, and despairing squeals were wafted to me, so I presumed that it must have run straight into the net. Shouting for the hunters, I struggled through the long grass towards the spot where the net was moving.

CANE RAT

Our quarry had entangled itself very thoroughly. Peering
at it, I could see we had caught a very large cane rat, a creature
known to the Africans as a cutting-grass, a name that describes
its habits very well, for with its large, well-developed incisors
the cutting-grass goes through the grassfields—and the farm-
lands—like a mowing machine. It measured about two and a
half feet in length and was covered with a coarse brownish-
coloured fur. It had a chubby, rather beaver-like face, small
ears set close to the head, a thick naked tail, and large naked
feet. It seemed so scared of my presence that I did not approach
it until the hunters arrived, for fear it would break out of the
net. It lay there quivering violently, occasionally giving little
jerks and leaps into the air accompanied by despairing squeals.
At the time this action worried me quite a lot, for it looked
as though the creature was in the last stages of a heart attack.

It was only later, when I grew to know these animals better, that I discovered they greeted any unusual experience with this display of hysteria, in the hope, I suppose, of frightening or confusing the enemy. In reality, cane rats are not very timid and would not hesitate to bury their large incisors in the back of your hand if you tried to take liberties with them. But, as I say, I did not know this at the time, and so I kept a discreet distance until the hunters joined me; then we went forward and removed the rat from the net.

While we were manoeuvring it from the net into a stout bag it suddenly jumped violently in my hands; to my surprise, as I tightened my grip, a large quantity of fur came away in my fingers. When we had it safely in the bag I sat down and examined the hair my clutch had removed from the fat body: it was fairly long and quite thick, more like a coarse bristle; apparently it is planted so loosely in the skin that it comes away in handfuls at the slightest pull. Once it has come away, the hair takes an incredibly long time to grow again, and, as bald cane rats are not exactly prepossessing, one had to handle them with extreme caution.

After we had captured the cane rat we made our way slowly up the valley, spreading the net at intervals and beating likely-looking patches of undergrowth. When it was obvious that the valley would yield nothing more in the way of specimens we rolled up the nets and headed for a large hill about half a mile away. This hill was so beautifully formed that it might well have been a barrow, the grave of some giant who had prowled the grassland in days gone by. On the very top was a cluster of boulders, each the size of a house, rearing up like a monument. In the narrow crevices and gullies between the rocks tiny trees were growing, their trunks twisted and crumpled by the winds, each bearing bright golden fruit. In the long grass round the base of the trunks grew small purple and yellow orchids, and in places the great rocks were covered with a thick mat of climbing plant, a form of convolvulus, from which dangled the ivory-coloured trumpet-shaped flowers. The great pile of rocks, the bright flowers, and the shaggy, misshapen trees formed a wonderful picture against the smouldering blue of the afternoon sky.

We climbed up into the shade of the rocks and squatted in the long grass to have our meal. The mountain grassland spread away from us in all directions, its multitude of colours shimmering and changing with the wind. The hill crests were pale gold changing to white, while the valleys were pale greeny-blue, darker in places where a pompous cumulus cloud swept over, trailing a purple shadow in its wake. Directly ahead of us lay a long range of delicately sculptured hills whose base was almost hidden in a litter of great boulders and small trees. The hills, clad in grass that showed a bewildering variety of greens, golds, purples and whites, were so smoothly and beautifully formed that they looked like a great rambling wave rearing up to break over the puny breakwater of rocks and shrubs below. The peace and silence of these heights were remarkable; nearly all sounds were created by the wind, which was busily moving here and there, making each object produce its own song. It combed the grass and brought forth a soft lisping rustle; it squeezed and wriggled between the cracks and joints of the rocks above us and made owl-like moans and sudden hoots of mirth; it pushed and wrestled with the tough little trees, making them creak and groan, and making their leaves flutter and

purr like kittens. Yet all these small sounds seemed to enhance
rather than destroy the silence of the grassland.

Suddenly the quiet was shattered by a terrific uproar that
broke out behind the massive pile of rocks. Working my way
round, I found the hunters and dogs in a group at the base of
a giant rock. Three of the hunters were arguing vigorously,
and the fourth was dancing about, scattering large quantities
of blood from a wound in his hand and yelping with pain.
The excited dogs leaped and barked frenziedly around him.

"Na whatee dis palaver?" I asked.

All four turned on me and offered their separate descriptions
of the event, their voices becoming louder and louder as they
tried to shout one another down.

"Why you all de shout? How I go hear if you all go talk
together like women, eh?" I said. Having thus produced silence, I pointed at the bloodstained hunter. "Now, how you
done get dis wound, ma friend?"

"Masa, beef done chop me."

"Beef? What kind of beef?"

"Eh! Masa, I no savvay. 'E de bite too much, sah."

I examined his hand and found that a chunk the size of a
shilling had been neatly removed from the palm. I rendered
primitive first aid and then went into the matter of the animal
that had bitten him.

"Which side dis beef?"

" 'E dere dere for dat hole, sah," said the wounded one, pointing at a cleft in the base of a large rock.

"You no savvay what kind of beef?"

"No, sah," he said aggrievedly, "I no see um. I go come for
dis place an' I see dat hole. I tink sometime dere go be beef

for inside so I done put ma hand for dere. Den dis beef 'e done chop me."

"Whah! Dis man no get fear," I said, turning to the other hunters. "He no go look de hole first. He done put his hand for inside and beef done chop him."

The other hunters giggled. I turned to the wounded man again. "Ma friend, you done put your hand for dis hole, eh? Now, sometimes you go find snake for dis kind of place, no be so? If snake done chop you, what you go do?"

"I no savvay, Masa," he said, grinning.

"I no want dead hunter man, ma friend, so you no go do dis sort of foolish thing again, you hear?"

"I hear, sah."

"All right. Now we go look dis beef that done chop you."

I took a torch from the collecting bag, crouched down by the hole, and peered up it. In the beam a pair of small eyes glowed ruby red, and then a small, pointed ginger-coloured face appeared round them, uttered a shrill, snarling screech, and disappeared into the gloom at the back of the hole.

"Ah," said one of the hunters who had heard the noise, "dis na bush dog! Dis beef 'e fierce too much, sah."

Unfortunately the pidgin-English term "bush dog" is used indiscriminately to describe a great variety of small mammals, few of which are even remotely related to dogs, so the hunter's remark left me none the wiser as to what sort of an animal it was. After some argument we decided that the best way to get the beast to show itself was to light a small fire outside the hole and blow the smoke into it by fanning with a bunch of leaves. This we proceeded to do, having first hung a small net over the mouth of the hole.

The first whiff of smoke had hardly drifted in among the rocks when the beast shot out of the hole and into the net with such force that the net was torn from its moorings, and the animal rolled down the slope into the long grass, carrying the net with it. The dogs scrambled after it, barking with excitement, and we followed close on their heels, yelling threats as to what punishment they would receive if they harmed the quarry. However, the beast hardly needed our help, for it was perfectly capable of looking after itself, as we soon found out. It shook itself free of the folds of netting and rose up on its hind legs, revealing itself as a small, slim ginger-coloured mongoose about the size of a stoat. It stood there swaying slightly from side to side, its mouth wide open, uttering the most ear-piercing shrieks I have ever heard from an animal of that size. The dogs pulled up short and surveyed it in consternation. One, slightly braver than the rest, moved forward gingerly and sniffed at the strange creature—which was what the mongoose had been waiting for. It dropped flat in the grass and slid forward like a snake, disappearing among the long grass stalks and then suddenly reappearing in between the feet of our noble pack, where it proceeded to whirl like a top, biting at every paw and leg in sight and screaming incessantly as it did so. The dogs did their best to avoid its jaws, but they were at a disadvantage, for the long grass hid the mongoose's approach, and so all they could do was leap wildly in the air. Then, suddenly, their courage failed them, and they all turned tail and fled up the hill, leaving the mongoose standing on its hind legs in the field of battle, panting slightly, but still able to screech taunts at their retreating tails.

The pack having thus been vanquished, it was left to us to

MONGOOSE

try to capture this fierce, if diminutive, adversary. This we
accomplished more easily than I had thought possible. I attracted its attention and got it to attack a canvas collecting bag,
while one of the hunters crept round behind and threw a net
over it. During the time we were disentangling the mongoose
from the net and getting it into a bag, it nearly deafened us
with screams of rage, and this ghastly noise continued all the
way home, though mercifully slightly muffled by the thick
canvas. The mongoose did not stop until, on reaching Bafut,
I tipped it into a large cage and threw in a gory chicken's
head. It settled down to eat this in a very philosophical manner
and had very soon finished. After that it remained silent, ex-

cept on catching sight of anyone, when it would rush to the bars and start to scream abuse. This became so nerve-racking that I was forced to cover the front of the cage with a bit of sacking until it had become more used to human company. Three days later I heard those familiar screeches echoing down the road, and long before the native hunter appeared in sight I knew that another dwarf mongoose was being brought in. I was pleased to find that this second one was a young female, so I put her in with the one we had captured. This was rather unwise of me, for they took to screaming in chorus, each trying to outdo the other, until the noise had all the soothing qualities of a knife drawn sideways across a plate, magnified several thousand times.

On arrival back at Bafut, after my first day out with the Beagles, I received a note from the Fon asking me to go over to his house for a drink and to give him any hunting news there might be. When I had eaten and changed I walked across the great courtyard and came to the Fon's little villa. He was seated on the veranda, holding a bottle of gin up to the light to see what the contents were.

"Ah, ma friend!" he said. "You done come? You done have good hunting for bush?"

"Yes," I said, taking the chair he offered. "Hunter man for Bafut savvay catch fine beef. We done catch three beef."

"Foine, foine," said the Fon, pouring five fingers of gin into a glass and handing it to me. "You go stay here small time you go get plenty plenty beef. I go tell all ma peoples."

"Na so. I think Bafut people savvay catch beef pass all people for Cameroons."

"Na true, na true," said the Fon delightedly. "You speak true, ma friend."

We raised our glasses, clinked them, beamed at each other, and drank deeply. The Fon refilled the glasses, then sent one of his numerous retinue in search of a fresh bottle. By the time we had worked our way through it we had mellowed considerably.

"You like musica?" the Fon inquired.

"Yes, too much," I said truthfully, for I heard that the Fon possessed a band of more than usual skill.

"Good! We go have some musica," he said and issued a terse command to one of his servants.

Presently the band filed into the compound below the veranda, and, to my surprise, it consisted of about twenty of the Fon's wives, all naked except for small loincloths. They were armed with a tremendous variety of drums, ranging in size from a small saucepan to the deep-bellied specimens that require two people to carry them. There were also wooden and bamboo flutes, which had a curious sweetness of tone, and large bamboo boxes filled with dried maize that gave forth a wonderful rustling rattle when shaken. But the most curious instrument in the band was a wooden pipe about four feet long. This was held upright, with one end resting on the ground, and blown into in a special way, producing a deep, vibrating noise that was rather astonishing, for it was the sort of sound you would expect to emanate only from a lavatory with exceptional acoustic properties.

The band began to play, and soon various members of the Fon's household were dancing in the compound. It was a cross between folk dancing and ballroom dancing. The couples,

clasping each other, gyrated slowly round and round, their feet
performing tiny and complicated steps, while their bodies wiggled and swayed in a way that no Palais de Danse would have
allowed. Occasionally a couple broke apart and each twirled
off on his own for a time, doing his own swaying steps to the
music, completely absorbed. The flutes twittered and squeaked,
the drums galloped and shuddered, the rattles crashed and rus-
tled with the monotonous regularity of waves on a shingle
beach, and steadily, behind this frenzy of sound, you could hear
the tubalike instrument's cry, a gigantic catharsis every few
seconds with the consistancy of a heartbeat.

"You like my musica?" shouted the Fon.

"Yes, na very fine," I roared back.

"You get dis kind of musica for your country?"

"No," I said with genuine regret, "we no get um."

The Fon filled my glass again. "Soon, when my people bring
grass, we go have plenty musica, plenty dancing, eh? We go
have happy time. We go be happy too much, no be so?"

"Yes, na so. We go have happy time."

Outside in the compound the band played on, and the steady
roll and thud of the drums seemed to drift up into the dark sky
and make even the stars shiver and dance to their rhythm.

3. THE SQUIRREL THAT BOOMS

There were two species of grassland fauna that I was very anxious to obtain during my stay in Bafut: one was the rock hyrax,
and the other was Stanger's squirrel. To get them I had to un-
dertake two hunts in widely different types of country, and
they remain in my mind more vividly than almost any other
hunting experiences I had in the grasslands.

The first of these hunts was after the squirrel, and it was remarkable chiefly for the fact that it was one of the very few
occasions when I have been able to plan a campaign in advance
and carry it through successfully without any last minute, un-
foreseen hitches ruining it. Stanger's squirrel is a reasonably
common animal in the Cameroons, but previously I had hunted
for it in the deep forest in the Mamfe basin. In this sort of country it spends its time in the top branches of the higher trees,
feeding on the rich banquet of fruit growing in those sunny
heights, and rarely coming down to ground level, which makes

its capture almost impossible. I had since learned that in the grassland the squirrel frequents the small patches of forest on riverbanks and spends quite a large part of its time on the ground, foraging in the grass for food. This, I felt, would give me a better chance.

When I showed a picture of the squirrel to the Bafut Beagles they identified it immediately and vociferously maintained that they knew where it was to be found. Questioning them, I found that they knew the habits of the creature quite well, for they had hunted it on numerous occasions. Apparently the squirrels lived in a small patch of mountain forest, but in the very early morning or in the evening they came down from the trees and ventured into the grassland to feed. That, said the Bafut Beagles, was the time to catch them. What, I asked, did this beef do during the night?

"Ah! Masa, you no fit catch um for nighttime," came the reply. "Dis beef 'e de sleep for up dat big stick where no man fit pass. But for evening time, or early early morning time, we fit catch um."

"Right," I said, "we go catch um for early early morning time."

We left Bafut at one o'clock in the morning, and after a long and tedious walk over hills, through valleys and grassfields, we reached our destination an hour before dawn. It was a small plateau lying halfway up a steep mountainside. The area was comparatively flat, and across it tinkled a wide, shallow stream along the sides of which grew a thick but narrow strip of forest. Crouching in the lee of a big rock, peering into the gloom, and wiping the dew from our faces, we spied out the land and made our plans. The idea was to erect two or three strips of net in the long grass about five hundred yards away from the edge of the trees. This we had to do immediately, before it was light enough for the squirrels to see us. Erecting nets in grass sodden with dew, that is up to your waist, is not a soothing pastime, and we were glad when the last one had been tied in place. Then we cautiously approached the forest and crawled into hiding beneath a large bush. Here we squatted, trying to keep our teeth from chattering, not able to smoke or talk or move.

The eastern sky grew paler as the darkness of the night was drained out of it and slowly turned to pale opalescent grey; then it flushed to pink, and then, as the sun rose above the horizon, it turned suddenly and blindingly to a brilliant kingfisher blue. This pure, delicate light showed the mountains around us in low-lying mist; as the sun rose higher, the mist started to move and slide on the ridges and pour down the hillsides to fill the valleys. For one brief instant we had seen the grasslands quiet and asleep under the blanket of mist; now it seemed as though the mountains were awakening, yawning and stretching under the white coverlet, pushing it aside in some places, gathering it more tightly in others, hoisting itself dew-misted and sleepy from the depths of its white bedclothes.

I watched this awakening of the mountains many times and never wearied of the sight. Considering that the same thing has been happening each morning since the ancient mountains came into being, it is astonishing how fresh and new the sight appears each time you witness it. Never does it become dull and mechanical; it is always different. Sometimes the mist in rising shapes itself into strange animal forms—dragons, phoenix, wyvern, and milk-white unicorns—or into strange, drifting strands of seaweed, trees, or great tumbling bushes of white flowers. Occasionally, if there is a breeze to help, it startles you by assuming severe and complicated geometrical shapes. All the while, underneath it, in tantalizing glimpses as it shifts, you can see the mountains gleaming in a range of soft colourings so delicate and ethereal that it is impossible to put a name to them.

I decided as I squatted there, peering between the branches of the sheltering bush, that it was worth feeling tired, cold, and hungry, worth being drenched with dew and suffering cramps, in order to see the mountains awaken. My meditations were interrupted by a loud and aggresive "chuck, chuck" from the trees above us, and one of the hunters gripped my arm and looked at me with glowing eyes. He leaned forward slowly and whispered in my ear, "Masa, dis na de beef Masa want. We go sit softly softly 'e go come down for ground small time."

I wiped the dew from my face and looked out at the grassfield where we had set the nets. Presently we heard other chucking noises from deeper in the forest as more of the squirrels awoke and glanced at the day with suspicious eyes. We waited for what seemed a long time, and then I suddenly saw something moving in the grassfield between us and the nets, a curious object, which at first sight looked like an elongated black-and-white-striped balloon, appearing now and then above the long grass. In that mist-blurred morning haze I could not make out what this could be, and so I attracted the hunters' attention and pointed to it silently.

"Dis na de beef, Masa," said one.

" 'E done go for ground, 'e done go for ground," said another gleefully.

"Na whatee dat ting?" I whispered, for I could not reconcile that balloonlike object with any part of a squirrel's anatomy.

SQUIRRELS

"Dis ting na 'e tail, sah," explained a hunter, and, so that I should be left in no doubt, he added, "Dat ting 'e get for 'e larse."

Like all tricks, once it had been explained it became obvious. I could see quite clearly that the black-and-white-striped object *was* a squirrel's tail, and I wondered why on earth I had thought that it resembled a balloon. Soon the one tail was joined by others, and as the mist lifted and cleared we could see the squirrels themselves.

There were eight of them hopping out into the grassfield. They were large, rather bulky animals with heavy heads, but the largest and most flamboyant part of their anatomies were their tails. They hopped cautiously from tussock to tussock, pausing to sit up on their hind legs and to sniff carefully in the direction they were travelling. Then they would get down and hop forward a few more feet, flipping their tails as they moved. Sometimes they would crouch perfectly still for a few seconds, their tails laid carefully over their backs, the bushy ends hanging down and almost obscuring their faces. The ones in the grassfield were silent, but in the trees behind us we could still hear an occasional suspicious "chuck" from the ones that had not yet plucked up the courage to descend.

I decided that eight would be quite enough for us to try to catch, so I signalled the hunters and we rose from our hideout. When we were spread out in a line through the trees the hunters paused and waited for the signal to advance. The squirrels were now about a hundred and fifty yards from the forest's edge, and this was far enough for our purposes. I waved my hand, and we walked out from the shelter of the trees into the long grass. The squirrels in the forest gave loud chucks of alarm, and the squirrels in the grassfield sat up on their hind legs to see what was the matter. They saw us and froze instantly. As we moved slowly forward they hopped off into the grass, farther and farther from the trees. I don't think they could quite make out what we were, for we moved very slowly and with the minimum of movement. They felt we were something hostile but they were not certain; they would run a few yards and then stop and sit up to survey us, sniffing vigorously. This was really the most ticklish part of the capture, for the animals were not yet within the semicircle of the nets, and by breaking away to left or right they could easily escape. We drifted towards them cautiously. The only sounds were the swish of our feet in the grass and the faint, frantic chucks from the forest behind us.

One squirrel was more quick-witted than the rest. He could not see the nets ahead, for they were hidden in the long grass and well camouflaged, but he suddenly realized that as we advanced we were driving him farther and farther from the forest and the safety of the tall trees. He gave a loud chuck of alarm and dashed off through the grass, his long tail streaming out behind him, and then suddenly twisted to the left and galloped through the grass away from the nets. His one ambition was to get round us and back to the trees. The rest of the squirrels sat up and watched him nervously, and I realized that unless something was done they would all pluck up courage and follow his example. I had planned to wait until they were well within the circle of nets before charging down on them and causing a panic that would send them scuttling into the mesh, but we had to take the chance and stampede them now. I raised my hand, and the hunters and I surged forward, yelling and hooting, waving our arms and trying to appear as fearsome as possible. For a split second the squirrels watched us without moving, then they fled.

Four of them followed the example of the first and dashed off at right angles, avoiding both the hunters and the nets; the remaining three ran straight for our trap, and as we ran towards the scene we could see the top of the net jerking, an indication that they had got themselves tangled up. Sure enough, we found them firmly entwined, glaring out at us and giving vent to the loudest gurking noises I ever heard from a squirrel. It was a sound completely different from the loud chuck they had been making: it was fearsome and full of warning—a cross between a snore and a snarl. While we were unwinding them they kept this up, along with biting savagely at our hands with their large orange incisors. When we had at last got them into canvas bags we had to hang the bags on the end of a stick to carry them; for, unlike other grassland squirrels, which lie quietly when put in the gloom of a bag, these creatures seemed quite willing to continue the fight, and the slightest touch on the outside of the bag would be greeted by a furious attack and a rapid series of gurks.

The squirrels in the forest were thoroughly alarmed, and the trees echoed to the sound of frantic chuckings. Now that they had realized how dangerous we were it was useless to attempt another capture, so we had to be content with the three we had caught. We packed up our nets and other equipment and made our way back to Bafut.

Once there, I placed my precious squirrels in three solid, tin-lined cages, filled their plates with food, and left them severely alone until they should have recovered from the indignity of capture. As soon as they were alone they ventured out of the

darkness of their bedrooms and demolished the piles of succulent fruits I had provided, upset their water pots, tested the tin
linings of the cages to see if they could be gnawed through, and,
finding that it was impossible, retired to their bedrooms again
and slept.

At close quarters they were quite handsome beasts, with pale
yellow bellies and cheeks, russet-red backs, and huge striped
tails. The effect was somewhat spoiled by their heads, which
were large and rather horsy, with tiny ears set close to the
skulls and protuberant teeth.

I had read somewhere that these squirrels climb to the top
branches of the forest trees in the early morning and give vent
to the most powerful and astonishing cries: a deep rolling sound
like the last notes of a giant gong being struck. I wanted to hear
this, but I thought it unlikely that they would produce it in
captivity. However, the morning after their capture I was
awakened at about five-thirty by a peculiar noise—the collection was on the veranda outside my window—and on sitting up
in bed I decided that the noise was coming from one of the
cages, but I could not tell from which one. I put on my dressing
gown and crept out of the door. Chilly and half awake, I waited
patiently in the dim light for a repetition of the sound. It came
again in a few minutes, and I could definitely trace it to the
squirrels. The noise was extremely difficult to describe: it
started like a groan, and as it got louder it took on a throbbing,
vibrating note, the sort of thrumming you hear from telegraph
poles. The sound seemed to blur and waver, like a gong hit very
softly, rising to a crescendo and then dying away. The squirrels
were obviously being rather halfhearted about their attempt;
in the forest they would have put much more force into it, and

then, I should imagine, it would be a weird, fascinating cry to
hear as it drifted through the misty branches of the trees.

That evening the Fon appeared, as usual, to find out what
success the day had brought and to present me with a calabash
of fresh palm wine. With great pride I showed him the squirrels
and described the capture in detail. He wanted to know exactly
where we had caught them, and as I did not really know I had to
call one of the hunters, who was merrymaking in the kitchen, to
explain to him. He stood in front of the Fon, answering his
questions through cupped hands. It took quite a long time, for
the locality was uninhabited, and the hunter could describe our
route only by reference to various landmarks in the shape of
rocks, trees, and curiously shaped hills. At last the Fon nodded
vigorously. For a few minutes he sat lost in thought, then he
spoke to the hunter rapidly, making wide gestures with his long
arms, while the hunter nodded and bowed.

When this was over the Fon turned to me, smiling benignly,
and carelessly, almost absent-mindedly, holding out his empty
glass. "I done tell dis man," he explained, watching me fill the
glass with apparent disinterest, " 'e go take you for some special
place for mountain. For dis place you get some special kind of
beef."

"What kind of beef?"

"Beef," said the Fon vaguely, gesturing with his half-empty
glass. "Special kind of beef. You no get um yet."

"Na bad beef dis?" I suggested.

The Fon put his glass on the table and spread out his enormous hands. "Na so big," he said. "No be bad bad beef, but 'e
bite too much. 'E go live for dat big big rock, 'e go go for under.
Sometime 'e de hollar too much—'e go wheeeeeeeeee!"

I sat and puzzled over what the creature might be while the Fon watched me hopefully. " 'E look same same for cutting-grass, but 'e no get tail for 'e larse," he said.

Light suddenly dawned, and I went in search of a book. I found the picture I wanted and showed it to the Fon. "Dis na de beef?" I asked.

"Ah! Na so," said the Fon delightedly, stroking the picture of the rock hyrax. "Dis na de beef. How you call um?"

"Rock hyrax."

"Rooke hyrix?"

"Yes. How you de call um for Bafut?"

"Here we call um n'eer."

I wrote the name down on the list of local names I was compiling, then refilled the Fon's glass. He was still gazing in a trance at the engraving, tracing the outline of the hyrax with one slender finger.

"Whah!" he said in a wistful voice. "Na fine chop dis beef. You go cook um with cocoa yam . . ." His voice died away, and he licked his lips reminiscently.

The hunter fixed me with his eyes and shuffled his feet as an indication that he wanted to speak.

"Yes, na whatee?"

"Masa want to go for dis place de Fon de talk?"

"Yes. We go go tomorrow for morning time."

"Yes, sah. For catch dis beef Masa go need plenty people. Dis beef fit run too much, sah."

"All right. You go tell all my boys dey go for bush tomorrow."

"Yes, sah."

He stood and shuffled his feet again.

"Whatee?"

"Masa go want me again?"

"No, my friend. Go back for kitchen and drink your wine."

"Tank you, sah," he said, grinning, and disappeared into the gloom of the veranda.

When the Fon rose to go I walked with him as far as the road. At the edge of the compound he turned and smiled down at me from his great height. "I be ole man," he said, "I de tire too much. If I no be ole man I go come with you for bush tomorrow."

"You lie, my friend. You no be ole man. You done get plenty power—power pass all dis picken hunter man."

He chuckled, then sighed. "No, my friend, you no speak true. My time done pass. I de tire too much. I get plenty wife, and dey de tire me too much. I get palaver with dis man, with dat man, an' it de tire me too much. Bafut na big place, plenty people. If you get plenty people you get plenty palaver."

"Na so, I savvay you get plenty work."

"True," he said, and then added, his eyes twinkling, "Sometimes I get palaver with the D.O., an' dat de tire me most of all."

He shook my hand, and I could hear him chuckling as he walked off across the courtyard.

The next morning we set off on our hyrax hunt—myself, the four Bafut Beagles, and five of the household staff. For the first two or three miles we walked through the cultivated areas and the small farms. On the gently sloping hills small fields had been dug, and the rich red earth shone in the early morning sunshine. The crops were already planted and ripening, the feathery bushes of cassava and the rows of maize, each golden head with its blond tassel of silken thread waving in the breeze. Women were at work in the fields, stripped to the waist, wielding the short-handled, broad-bladed hoes. Some had tiny babies strapped to their backs, and they seemed as unaware of these encumbrances as a snail of its shell. The older ones smoked long black pipes, and the rank grey smoke swirled up into their faces as they bent over the ground. It was mostly the younger women who were doing the harder work of hoeing, and their lithe, glistening bodies moved rhythmically in the sun as they raised the heavy, clumsy implements high above their heads and brought them sweeping down. Each time the blade buried itself in the red earth the owner would give a loud grunt. As we walked through the fields among them they talked with us in their shrill voices, made jokes, and laughed uproariously, without once pausing in their work or losing its rhythm. The grunts that interspersed their remarks gave a curious sound to the conversation.

"Morning, Masa . . . ugh! Which side you go? . . . ugh!" "Masa go go for bush . . . ugh! No be so Masa? . . . ugh!" "Masa go catch plenty beef . . . ugh! Masa get power . . . ugh!" "Walker strong, Masa . . . ugh! Catch beef *plenty* . . . ugh!" Long after we had left the fields and were scrambling up the golden slopes of the foothills we could hear the chattering and laughing and the steady thump of the hoes striking home.

When we reached the crest of the highest range of hills that surrounded Bafut the hunters pointed out our destination, a range of mountains, purple and misty, that seemed an incredible distance away. The household staff gave vent to gasps and moans of dismay and astonishment that I should want them to walk so far, and Jacob, the cook, said he didn't think he would be able to manage it, as he had unfortunately picked up a thorn in his foot. Examination proved that this was not a thorn in his foot but a small stone in his shoe. The discovery and removal of this left him moody and disgruntled, and he lagged behind, talking to himself in a ferocious undertone.

The distance was deceptive, and within three hours we were walking up a long winding valley at the end of which the mountains reared up in a wall of glittering gold and green. As we toiled up the slope through the waist-high grass the hunters explained what the plan of campaign was to be. Apparently we had to round one of the smoothly shaped buttresses of the mountain range, and in between this projection and the next lay a long valley that thrust its way into the heart of the mountains. The sides of the valley were almost sheer cliffs, at the base of which were the rocks where the hyrax lived.

We scrambled round the great elbow of mountain, and there lay the valley before us, quiet and remote and filled with sparkling sunlight that lit the gaunt cliffs on each side, two long crumpled curtains of rock flushed to pink and grey, patched with golden sunlight and soft blue shadows. Piled at the base of the cliffs were the legacies of many past falls and landslides, a jumble of boulders of all shapes and sizes, some scattered about the curving floor of the valley, some piled up into tall tottering chimneys. Over and around these rocks grew a rippling green rug of short undergrowth, long grass, hunched, crafty-looking trees, small orchids and tall lillies, and a thick, strangling web of convolvulus with yellow, cream, and pink flowers. Scattered along the cliff faces were a series of cave mouths, dark and mysterious, some mere narrow clefts in the rock, others the size of a cathedral door. Down the centre of the valley a boisterous baby stream wiggled joyfully in and out of the rocks and impatiently leaped in lacy waterfalls from one level to the next as it hurried down the slope.

We paused at the head of the valley for a rest and a smoke, and I examined the rocks ahead with my field glasses for any signs of life. But the valley seemed lifeless and deserted; the only sounds were the important and rather ridiculous tinkle of the diminutive stream, and the wind and the grass moving together and discussing our arrival in stealthy sibilant whispers. High overhead a small hawk appeared against the delicate blue sky, paused for an instant, and swept out of view behind the jagged edge of the cliff.

Jacob surveyed the valley with a sour expression on his pudgy countenance.

"Na whatee, Jacob?" I asked innocently. "You see beef?"

"No, sah," he said, glowering at his feet.

"You no like dis place?"

"No, sah, I no like um."

"Why?"

"Na bad place dis, sah."

"Why na bad place?"

"Eh! Sometime for dis kind of place you get bad juju, Masa."

I looked at the Bafut Beagles who were lying in the grass. "You get juju for dis place?" I asked them.

"No, sah, attall," they said unanimously.

"You see," I said to Jacob, "dere no be juju for here, so you no go fear, you hear?"

"Yes, sah," said Jacob with complete lack of conviction.

"And if you go catch dis beef for me I go give you fine dash," I went on.

Jacob brightened visibly. "Masa go give us dash same same for hunter man?" he asked hopefully.

"Na so."

He sighed and scratched his stomach thoughtfully.

"You still think dere be juju for dis place?"

"Eh!" he said, shrugging. "Sometime I done make mistake."

"Ah, Jacob, if Masa go give you dash you go kill your own mammy," said one of the Bafut Beagles, chuckling, for Jacob's preoccupation with money was well known in Bafut.

"Whah," said Jacob angrily, "an' you no love money, eh? Why you go come for bush with Masa if you no love money, eh?"

"Na my job," said the hunter, and added by way of explanation, "I be Beagle."

Before Jacob could think up a suitable retort one of the other hunters held up his hand. "Listen, Masa!" he said excitedly.

We all fell silent. From the valley ahead a strange cry drifted down to us. It started as a series of short, tremulous whistles, delivered at intervals, and then suddenly turned into a prolonged hoot that echoed weirdly from the rocky walls of the valley.

"Na n'eer dis, Masa," the Beagles whispered. " 'E de hollar for dat big rock dere."

I trained my field glasses on the big huddle of rocks they indicated, but it was some seconds before I saw the hyrax. He was squatting on a ledge of rock, surveying the valley with a haughty expression on his face. He was about the size of a large rabbit, but with short thick legs and a rather blunt lion-like face. His ears were small and neat, and he appeared to have no tail at all. As I watched, he turned on the narrow ledge

ROCK HYRAX

and ran to the top of the rock, paused for a moment to judge the distance, leaped lightly to the next pile of boulders, and disappeared into a tangle of convolvulus that obviously masked a hole of some sort. I lowered the glasses and looked at the Bafut Beagles.

"Well," I asked, "how we go catch dis beef?"

They had a rapid exchange of ideas in their own language. Then one of them turned to me. "Masa," he said, screwing up his face and scratching his head, "dis beef 'e clever too much. We no fit catch him with net, and 'e fit run pass man."

"Well, my friend, how we go do?"

"We go find hole for rock, sah, and we go make fire with

plenty smoke. We go put net for de hole, an' when de beef run, so we go catch um."

"All right," I said, "come, we go start."

We started off up the valley, Jacob leading the way with a look of grim determination on his face. We struggled through the thick web of short undergrowth until we reached the first tottering pile of boulders. There we spread out like terriers and scrambled and crawled our way round, peering into every crevice to see if it was inhabited.

It was Jacob, strangely enough, who first struck it lucky. He raised a sweaty, glowing face from the tangle of under-growth and called excitedly, "Masa, I done find hole! 'E get beef for inside!"

We crowded round the hole and listened. Sure enough, we could hear something stirring inside; faint scrabbling sounds were wafted to us. Rapidly we laid a fire of dried grass in the entrance to the hole, and when it was well alight we covered it with green leaves, which produced a column of thick, pun-gent smoke. We hung a net over the hole and then vigorously fanned the smoke into the depths of the rock with the aid of large bunches of leaves. The smoke rolled and tumbled up the tunnel into the darkness.

Suddenly things began to happen with bewildering rapidity. Two baby hyrax, each the size of a large guinea pig, shot out into the net with such force that they tore it down and rolled into the bushes with it tangled round them. Close on their heels came the mother, a corpulent beast in a towering rage. She raced out of the hole and leaped at the nearest person, who happened to be one of the Beagles. She moved so quickly that he had no time to get out of her way, and she fastened her teeth in his ankle and hung on like a bulldog, giving loud and terrifying "weeeeeeeee!" noises through her nose. The Beagle fell backwards into a great blanket of convolvulus. The other Beagles were busy trying to disentangle the baby hyrax from the net and were finding it a full-time job. The household staff had fled at the appearance of the irate mother, and so it was left to Jacob and me to go to the rescue of the Beagle who was lashing about in the undergrowth, screaming with pain at the top of his voice.

Before I could do anything sensible, however, Jacob came into his own. For the first and only occasion during the time I employed him his brain actually caught up with rapidly moving events. His action was not, I fear, the result of a sympathetic consideration for the sufferings of his fellow man but was prompted by the thought that unless something was done quickly the female hyrax might escape, in which case he would get no money for her. He leaped past me, with extraordinary speed for one normally so somnolent, clutching in his hand one of the larger canvas bags. Before I could stop him he had grabbed the unfortunate Beagle's leg and stuffed it into the bag, together with the hyrax. Then he drew the mouth of the bag tight with a smile of satisfaction and turned to me. "Masa!" he said, raising his voice above the indignant screams of his countryman, "I done catch um!"

His triumph, however, was short-lived, for the Beagle had come to the end of his patience, and he rose out of the under-growth and hit Jacob hard on the back of his woolly head. Jacob gave a roar of anguish and rolled backwards down the slope, while the Beagle rose to his feet and made desperate efforts to rid his foot of the hyrax-filled bag. I very much regret having to admit it, but I could do nothing more sensible than sit down on a rock and laugh until the tears ran down my face. Jacob rose to his feet, uttering loud threats, and saw the Beagle trying to remove the bag. "Arrrr!" he yelled, leaping up the slope. "Stupid man! De beef go run!" He clasped the Beagle in his arms, and they both fell backwards into the undergrowth.

By now the other Beagles had successfully bagged the other hyrax, and they came to the rescue. They dragged Jacob away and helped their fellow hunter remove the bag from his foot. Luckily the hyrax had released her hold on his foot when she was crammed into the bag, and had obviously become too frightened to bite again, but even so it must have been an unpleasant experience.

Still shaken with gusts of laughter, which I did my best to conceal, I administered first aid to the wounded Beagle and gave Jacob a good talking to, informing him that he would get only half the price of the capture, owing to his stupidity, and the other half would go to the hunter whose foot he had been so anxious to sacrifice. This decision was greeted with nods and grunts of satisfaction from everyone, including, strangely enough, Jacob himself. The average African, I have always found, has a remarkably well-developed sense of justice and will agree heartily with a fair verdict even if it is against himself.

With order restored, we went farther up the valley. After smoking out several caves and holes, with no results, we at last cornered and captured, without bloodshed on either side, a large male hyrax. I felt that four animals were more than my fair share of luck and that it would be a good idea to return home.

We wended our way out of the valley, along the edge of the mountain, and then down the gentle slopes of rolling golden grass towards Bafut. When we reached more or less level country we stopped for a smoke and a rest, and as we squatted in the warm grass I glanced back towards the mountains, my attention attracted by a low rumble of thunder. Unnoticed by us, a dark, heavy cloud had drifted across the sky and sprawled like a great shapeless Persian cat along the crest of the mountains. Its shadow changed the mountains from green and gold to an ugly purple, with harsh black stripes where the valleys lay. The cloud seemed to move, shifting and coiling within itself, and appeared to be padding and kneading the mountain crests like a cat on the arm of a gigantic chair. Occasionally a rent in the nebulous shape would be pierced by an arrow of sunlight, which would illuminate an area of the mountain below with a pure golden light, turning the grass to jade-green patches on the purple flanks of the mountains. With amazing rapidity the cloud grew darker and darker and seemed to swell as though gathering itself for a spring. Then the lightning began falling like jagged silver icicles, and the mountains shuddered with the vibrations of thunder.

"Masa, we go walka quick," said one of the Beagles. "Sometime dat storm go reach us."

We continued on our way as fast as we could, but we were not fast enough, for the cloud spilled over the mountaintop and spread over the sky behind us. A cold wind blew up, and close on its heels came the rain in an almost solid silver curtain. We were drenched within the first few seconds. The red earth turned dark and slippery, and the hiss of the rain in the grass made conversation almost impossible. By the time we reached the outskirts of Bafut our teeth were chattering and our sodden garments were sticking icily to us as we moved. As we reached the last stretch of road the rain dwindled to a fine, drifting spray, then ceased altogether, while a white mist rose from the wet earth and broke round our legs like the backwash of an enormous wave.

4.

THE KING AND THE CONGA

The great day of the grass-gathering ceremony arrived at last. Before dawn, when the stars had only just started to dwindle, before even the youngest and most enthusiastic village cockerel had tried his voice, I was awakened by the gentle throb of small drums, the laughter and chatter of shrill voices, and the soft scruff of bare feet on the dusty road below the house. I lay and listened to these sounds until the sky outside the window was faintly tinged with the green of the coming day, and then I went out on the veranda to see what was happening.

The mountains that clustered around Bafut were mauve and grey in the dim morning light, striped and patterned with deep purple and black in the valleys, where it was still night. The sky was magnificent, black in the west where the last stars quivered, jade green above me, fading to the palest kingfisher blue at the eastern rim of hills. I leaned against the wall of the veranda, where a great web of bougainvillia had grown like a carelessly

flung cloak of brick-red flowers, and looked down the long
flight of steps to the road below, and beyond it to the Fon's
great courtyard. Down the road, from both directions, came a
steady stream of people, laughing and talking and beating on
small drums when the mood took them. Over their shoulders
were long wooden poles, and tied to these with creepers were
great conical bundles of dried grass. The children trotted along
carrying smaller bundles on thin saplings. They made their
way down past the arched openings into the Fon's courtyard
and deposited the grass in heaps under the trees by the side of
the road. Having done this, they wended their way through the
arch into the courtyard, where they stood about in chattering
groups. Occasionally a flute and a drum would strike up a
brief melody, and then some of the crowd would break into a
shuffling dance, amid handclaps and cries of delight from the
onlookers. They were a happy, excited, and eager throng.

By the time I had finished breakfast the piles of grass bundles
by the roadside were towering skywards, threatening to over-
balance as each new lot was added. The courtyard was jammed
with people, and they overflowed through the arched door
and out into the road. The air was full of noise as the first arrivals greeted the latecomers and chaffed them for their laziness.
Children chased one another in and out of the crowd, shrieking
with laughter, and hordes of thin, scruffy dogs galloped joyfully at their heels, yelping enthusiastically. I walked down the
seventy-five steps to the road and joined the crowd. I was
pleased and flattered to find that they did not seem to resent
my presence among them but greeted me with quick, welcoming smiles that quickly turned to broad grins of delight when
I exchanged salutations in pidgin English. I took up a suitable

position by the roadside, in the shade of a huge hibiscus bush, scarlet with flowers and filled with the drone of insects. A circle of youths and children soon gathered round me, watching me silently as I sat and smoked and gazed at the gay crowd surging past. Eventually I was run to earth by a panting member of the household staff, who pointed out reproachfully that it was long past lunchtime and that the delicacy the cook had prepared would undoubtedly be ruined. Reluctantly I left my circle of disciples, who all stood up politely and shook my hand, and followed the grumbling Ben back to the house.

Having eaten, I descended once more to my vantage point beneath the hibiscus and continued my anthropological survey of the Bafut people as they streamed steadily past. Apparently, during the morning, I had been witnessing the arrival of the common or working man. These were, for the most part, dressed in gaudy sarongs twisted tightly round the hips. The women wore the same, though some of the very old ones had nothing but a dirty scrap of leather at the loins. This, I gathered, was the old style of costume; the bright sarong was a modern idea. Most of the older women smoked pipes, not the short stubby pipes common among the lowland tribes, but ones with long slender stems, like old-fashioned clay pipes, and these were black with use.

In the afternoon the council members, the petty chiefs, and other men of substance and importance started to arrive, and there was no mistaking them for just ordinary creatures of the soil. They all wore long, loose-fitting robes of splendid colours, which swished and sparkled as they walked, and on their heads were perched the little flat skullcaps I had noticed before, each embroidered with an intricate, colourful design.

Some carried long slender staves of a dark chocolate-coloured wood, covered with a surprisingly delicate tracery of carving. They were all middle-aged or elderly, obviously very conscious of their high office, and each greeted me with great solemnity, shaking me by the hand and saying "Welcome" several times in an earnest manner. There were a great many of these aristocrats, and they added a wonderful touch of colour to the proceedings.

When I went back to the house for tea I paused at the top of the steps and looked down at the great courtyard: it was a solid wedge of humanity packed so tightly together that the red earth was invisible, except in places where some happy dancers cleared a small circle by their antics. Scattered like flowers across a bed of black earth were the colourful robes of the elders.

Towards evening I was in the midst of the thickest part of the throng, endeavouring to take photographs before the light got too bad, when a resplendent figure made his appearance at my side. His robe glowed with magenta, gold, and green, and in one hand he held a long leather switch. He was the Fon's messenger, he informed me, and if I was quite ready he would take me to the Fon. The grass ceremony was about to begin. Hastily cramming another film into the camera, I followed him through the crowd, watching with admiration as he cleaved a way through the thickest part by the simple but effective method of slicing with his switch across the bare buttocks that presented themselves so plentifully on all sides. To my surprise, the crowd did not seem to take exception to this treatment but yelped and screamed in mock fear and pushed and stumbled out of our way, laughing with delight.

The messenger led me across the great courtyard, through the arched door, along a narrow passageway, and through another arched door that led into a honeycomb of tiny courtyards and passages. It was as complicated as a maze, but the messenger knew his way about. We ducked and twisted along passages, through courtyards, and up and down small flights of steps until at last we went through a crumbling brick archway and came out into an oblong courtyard about a quarter of an acre in extent, surrounded by a high red brick wall. At one end grew a large mango tree, and around its smooth trunk had been built a circular raised dais. On this was a large heavily carved chair in which sat the Fon of Bafut.

His clothing was so gloriously bright that for the moment I did not recognize him. His robe was a beautiful shade of sky blue, with a wonderful design embroidered on it in red, yellow, and white. On his head was a conical red felt hat to which had been stitched vast numbers of hairs from elephants' tails. From a distance he looked as though he were wearing a cone-shaped haystack on his head. In one hand he held a fly whisk: the handle of delicately carved wood and the swish made from the long, black and white tail of a colobus monkey—a thick silky plume of hair. The impressive effect was somewhat marred by the Fon's feet: they were resting on a huge elephant tusk—freckled yellow and black with age—that lay before him, and they were clad in a pair of very pointed piebald shoes, topped off by jade-green socks.

After he had shaken me by the hand and asked earnestly after my health a chair was brought for me, and I sat down beside him. The courtyard was lined with various councillors, petty chiefs, and their seminude wives, all of them squatting along the walls on their haunches, drinking out of carved horn flasks. The men's multicoloured robes made a wonderful tapestry along the red stone wall. To the left of the Fon's throne was a great pile of black calabashes, their necks stuffed with bunches of green leaves, containing mimbo, or palm wine, the most common drink in the Cameroons. One of the Fon's wives brought a glass for me, and then lifted one of the calabashes, removed the plug of leaves, and poured a drop of mimbo into the Fon's extended hand. He rolled the liquid round in his mouth thoughtfully, then spat it out and shook his head. Another flask was broached with the same result, and then two more. At last a calabash was found that contained mimbo the Fon considered fine enough to share with me, and the woman filled my glass. Mimbo looks like well-watered milk and has a mild, faintly sour, lemonade taste, which is most deceptive. A really good mimbo tastes innocuous, and thus lures you on to drink more and more, until suddenly you discover that it is not so harmless as you had thought. I tasted my glass of wine, smacked my lips, and complimented the Fon on the vintage. I noticed that all the councillors and petty chiefs were drinking out of flasks made from cows' horns, whereas the Fon was imbibing his mimbo from a beautifully carved and polished buffalo horn. We sat there until it was almost dark, talking and gradually emptying the calabashes of mimbo.

Eventually the Fon decided that the great moment for feeding the masses had arrived. We rose and walked down the courtyard between the double ranks of bowing subjects, the men clapping their hands rhythmically, the women holding their hands over their mouths, patting their lips and hooting,

FON OF BAFUT

producing a noise that I, in my innocence, had thought to be the prerogative of the Red Indian. We wended our way through the doors, passages, and tiny courtyards, and the congregation filed behind, still clapping and hooting. As we came out of the archway into the main courtyard there arose from the multitude a roar of approval that was deafening, accompanied by clapping and drumming. Amid this tumultuous reception the Fon and I walked along the wall to where the Fon's throne had been placed on a leopard skin. We took our seats, the Fon waved his hand, and the feast commenced.

Through the archway came an apparently endless stream of young men, naked except for small loincloths, carrying on their shining, muscular shoulders the various foods for the people. There were calabashes of palm wine and corn beer, huge bunches of plaintain and bananas, both green and golden yellow. There was meat in the shape of giant cane rats, mongooses, bats and antelope, monkeys and great hunks of python, all carefully smoked and spitted on bamboo poles. Then there were dried fish, dried shrimps, and fresh crabs, scarlet and green peppers, mangoes, oranges, pawpaws, pineapples, coconuts, cassava, and sweet potatoes.

While this incredible quantity of food was being distributed the Fon greeted all the head men, councillors, and chiefs. They would each approach him, bend double before him, and clap their hands three times. The Fon would give a brief and regal nod, and the man would retire backwards. If anyone wanted to address the Fon he had to do so through cupped hands.

I had by now absorbed quite a quantity of mimbo and was feeling more than ordinarily benign. It seemed to have much the same effect on the Fon. He barked a sudden order, and, to my horror, a table was produced on which reposed two glasses and a bottle of gin, a French brand I had never heard of and whose acquaintance I am not eager to renew. The Fon poured about three inches of gin into a glass and handed it to me. I smiled and tried to look as though gin, neat and in large quantities, was just what I had been wanting. I smelled the beverage gingerly—its odour resembled one of the finer brands of paraffin. Deciding that I really could not face such a large amount undiluted, I asked for some water. The Fon barked out another order, and one of his wives came running, clutching a bottle of Angostura in her hand.

"Beeters!" said the Fon proudly, shaking about two teaspoonfuls into my gin. "You like gin wit beeters?"

"Yes," I said with a sickly smile, "I love gin with bitters."

The first sip of the liquid nearly burned my throat out. It was quite the rawest of raw spirits I have ever tasted. Even the Fon, who did not appear to worry unduly about such things, blinked a bit after his first gulp. He coughed vigorously and turned to me, wiping his streaming eyes. "Very strong," he pointed out.

When all the food had been brought out and arranged in huge piles in front of us the Fon called for silence and made a short speech to the assembled Bafutians, telling them who I was, why I was there, and what I wanted. He ended by explaining that they had to procure plenty of animals for me. The crowd listened to the speech in complete silence, and when it had ended a chorus of loud "arhhh's!" broke loose, and much handclapping. The Fon sat down looking rather pleased with himself, and, carried away by his enthusiasm, he took a long swig at his gin. The result was an anxious five minutes for us all as he coughed and writhed on his throne, tears streaming down his face. He recovered eventually and sat there glaring at the gin in his glass with angry red eyes. He took another very small sip of it and rolled it round in his mouth, musing.

Then he leaned over to confide in me, "Dis gin strong too much. We go give dis strong drink to all dis small small men, den we go for my house and we drink, eh?"

I agreed that the idea of distributing the gin among the petty chiefs and councillors, the small small men, as the Fon called them, was an excellent one.

The Fon looked cautiously round to make sure we were not overheard. As there were only some five thousand people wedged around us he felt he could tell me a secret in complete safety. He leaned over and lowered his voice once more. "Soon we go for my house," he whispered gleefully. "We go drink White Horsh."

He sat back to watch the effect of his words on me. I rolled my eyes and tried to appear overcome with joy at the thought of this treat, while wondering what effect whisky would have on top of mimbo and gin. The Fon, however, seemed satisfied, and presently he called over the small small men, one by one, and poured the remains of the gin into their cow-horn drinking flasks, which were already half filled with mimbo. Never have I given up a drink so gladly. I wondered at the cast-iron stomachs that could face with equanimity, and even pleasure, a cocktail composed of that gin and mimbo.

Having distributed this rather doubtful largesse among his following, the Fon rose to his feet, amid handclaps, drumbeats, and Red Indian hootings, and led the way back through the intricate web of passages and courts until we came to his own small villa, almost hidden among his wives' many grass huts, like a matchbox in an apiary. We went inside, and I found myself in a large, low room furnished with easy chairs and a big table; the wooden floor was covered with fine leopard skins and highly coloured, locally made grass mats. The Fon, having done his duty to his people, relaxed in a long chair, and the whisky was produced. My host smacked his lips as the virginal bottle was uncorked and gave me to understand that, now the boring duties of state were over, we could start to drink in earnest. For the next two hours we drank steadily and discussed at great length and in the most complicated detail such fascinating topics as the best type of gun to use on an elephant, what White Horse was made of, why I didn't attend dinners at Buckingham Palace, the Russian question, and so on. After this neither the Fon's questions nor my answers had the skill and delicate construction we would have liked, so the Fon called for his band, being under the misguided impression that the ravages of strong drink could be dissipated by sweet music.

The band came into the courtyard outside and played and danced for a long time. To celebrate the arrival of the musicians the Fon insisted that another bottle of whisky be opened. Presently the band formed a semicircle, and a woman did a swaying, shuffling dance and sang in a shrill, doleful voice. I could not understand the words, but the song was incredibly mournful, and both the Fon and I were deeply affected by it. The Fon, wiping his eyes, sharply informed the band that they had better play something else. They held a long discussion among themselves and finally broke into a tune that was the most perfect conga rhythm imaginable. It was so bright and gay that it soon revived our spirits, and very soon I was tapping out the rhythm with my feet, while the Fon conducted the band with a glass of whisky clutched in one hand. Flushed with the Fon's hospitality and carried away by the tune, an idea came to me.

"The other night you done show me native dance, no be so?" I asked the Fon.

"Na so," he agreed, stifling a hiccup.

"All right. Tonight you like I go teach you European dance?"

"Ah! My friend," said the Fon, beaming and embracing me. "Yes, yes! Foine, you go teach me. Come, we go for dancing house."

We rose unsteadily to our feet and made our way to the dance hall. When we reached it, however, I found that the effort of walking fifty yards had told on my companion. He sank into his ornate throne with a gasp. "You go teach all dis small small men first," he said, gesturing wildly at the throng of chiefs and councillors. "Den I go dance."

I surveyed the shuffling, embarrassed crowd of council members that I was supposed to teach and decided that the more intricate steps of the conga—which was what I proposed to tutor them in—would be beyond them. Indeed, I was beginning to feel that they might even be beyond me. So I decided to content myself with showing them the latter part of the dance only, where everyone joins a line and does a sort of follow-the-leader round the place. The whole dance hall was hushed as I beckoned the two-and-twenty council members to join me on the floor, and in the silence you could hear their robes swishing as they walked. I made them join on behind me, each holding on to the waist of the man in front of him; then I gave a nod

to the band, who,
with great gusto, threw
themselves into the conga rhythm,
and we were off. I had carefully in-
structed the pupils to follow my every
movement, which they did. I soon discovered, however, that everything I knew about
the conga had been swamped by the Fon cel-
lars: all I could remember was that somewhere, sometime, one gave a kick.
So off we went, with the band playing frenziedly, round and round
the dance hall: one, two, three,
kick; one, two, three, kick.

My pupils had no difficulty in following this simple movement, and we went round the floor in great style, their robes swishing in unison. I was counting the beats and shouting "kick" at the appropriate moment, and apparently they took this to be part of the dance, a sort of religious chant that went with it, for they all started shouting in unison. The effect on our very considerable audience was terrific. Screeching with delight, various other members of the Fon's retinue, about forty of his wives, and several of his older offspring rushed to join the column of dancing councillors, and as each new dancer latched on to the tail he or she also joined the chant.

"One, two, three, keek!" yelled the councillors.

"One, two, three, *yarr*!" yelled the wives.

"On, doo, ree, *yarr*!" screeched the children.

The Fon was not going to be left out of this dance. He struggled up from his throne and, supported by a man on each side, tagged on behind. His kicks did not altogether coincide with the rhythmic movement of the rest of us, but he enjoyed himself nonetheless. I led them round and round the dance hall until I grew giddy, and the whole structure seemed to vibrate with the kicks and yells. Feeling that a little fresh air was indicated, I led them out of the door and into the open. Off we went in a tremendous, swaying line, up and down steps, in and out of courtyards, through strange huts, in fact everywhere that offered a free passage. The band, not to be outdone, followed us as we danced, running behind, sweating like mad, but never missing a beat. At last, more by luck than a sense of direction, I led my followers back into the dance hall, where we collapsed in a panting, laughing heap. The Fon, who had fallen down two or three times during the tour, was escorted back to his throne, beaming and gasping.

"Na foine dance dis," he proclaimed. "Foine, foine!"

"You like?" I asked, gulping for air.

"I like too much," said the Fon firmly. "You get plenty power. I never see European dance like dis."

I was not surprised. The average European one finds in West Africa does not spend his spare time teaching the conga to native chieftains and their courts. I have no doubt that, if they could have seen me in action, they would have informed me that I had done more damage to the white man's prestige in half an hour than anyone else had done in the whole history of the West Coast. However, my conga appeared to have increased my prestige with the Fon and his court.

"One, two, three, keek!" murmured the Fon reminiscently. "Na foine song dis."

"Na very special song," said I.

"Na so?" said the Fon, nodding his head. "Na foine one."

He sat on his throne and brooded for a while. The band struck up again and the dancers took the floor. I regained my breath and was beginning to feel rather proud of myself when my companion woke up suddenly and gave an order. A young girl of about fifteen left the dancers and approached the dais where we sat. Plump and shining with oil, she was clad in a minute loincloth that left few of her charms to the imagination. She sidled up to us, smiling shyly, and the Fon leaned forward and seized her by the wrist. With a quick pull and a twist he catapulted her into my lap, where she sat convulsed with giggles.

"Na for you, dis woman," said the Fon with a lordly wave of one enormous hand. "Na foine one. Na my daughter. You go marry her."

To say that I was startled means nothing; I was horror-stricken. My host was by now in that happy state that precedes belligerence, and I knew that my refusal would have to be put most tactfully, so that I would not undo the good work of the evening. I glanced round helplessly and noticed for the first time what an astonishing number of the crowd had spears with them. The band had stopped playing, and everyone was watching me expectantly. My host was regarding me, glassy-eyed. I had no means of telling whether he was really offering me the girl as a wife or whether this term was used as a euphemism for a more indelicate suggestion. Whichever it was, I had to refuse: quite apart from anything else, the girl was not my type. I licked my lips, cleared my throat, and did the best I could. I thanked the Fon graciously for his kind offer of the highly odiferous damsel—whose hundred and thirty odd pounds were at that moment making my knees ache—but, I said, since he was well versed in the stupid customs of my country, he knew it was impossible—however desirable—for me to have more than one wife. The Fon nodded wisely. Therefore, I went on, I was forced to refuse his extremely generous offer, for I already had one wife in England, and it would be unlawful, as well as unsafe, to take a second one back with me. If I had not already been married, I went on fluently, there was nothing I would have liked better than to accept his gift, marry the girl, and settle down in Bafut for the rest of my life.

To my great relief, a loud round of applause greeted my speech, and the Fon wept a bit that this lovely dream could never be realized. During the uproar I eased my dusky girl friend off my lap, gave her a slap on the rump, and sent her giggling back to the dance floor. Feeling that I had undergone quite enough for one night in the cause of diplomatic relations, I suggested that the party break up. The Fon and his retinue accompanied me to the great courtyard, where he insisted on clasping me round the waist and doing the Durrell conga once more. The crowd fell in behind, and we danced across the square, kicking and yelling, frightening the fruit bats out of the mango trees, and setting all the dogs barking for miles around. At the bottom of the steps the Fon and I bade each other a maudlin farewell, and I watched them doing an erratic conga back across the courtyard.

I climbed up the seventy-five steps, thinking longingly of bed, but was met at the top by a disapproving Ben with a hurricane lamp. "Sah, some hunter man done come," he said.

"What, at this hour?" I asked, surprised, for it was after three.

"Yes, sah. You want I tell um to go?"

"They done bring beef?" I asked hopefully, envisioning some rare specimen.

"No, sah. They want palaver with Masa."

"All right. Bring um," I said, sinking into a chair.

Ben ushered in five embarrassed young hunters, all clutching spears. They bowed and said good evening politely. They had been at the feast that night and had heard the Fon's speech; and, as they lived at a village some distance away, they thought they had better see me before they returned home, in order to find out exactly what kind of animals I wanted. I commended their zeal, distributed cigarettes, and brought out books and photographs. We pored over them for a long time, while I told them which creatures I particularly wanted and how much I was willing to pay. Just as they were about to go one young man noticed a drawing, which I had not shown them, lying on my bed.

"Masa want dis kind of beef?" he asked, pointing.

I peered at the drawing and then looked at the young man: he appeared to be quite serious about it. "Yes," I said emphatically, "I want dis kind of beef too much. Why, you savvay dis beef?"

"Yes, sah, I savvay um," said the hunter.

I held out the picture to the men. "Look um fine," I said.

They all stared at the bit of paper.

"Now for true, you savvay dis beef?" I asked again, trying to stifle my excitement.

"Yes, sah," they chorused, "we savvy um fine."

I gazed at them as though they were beings from another world. Their casual identification of the picture, coming so unexpectedly, had quite startled me, for the creature was one that I had long wanted to get hold of, perhaps the most remarkable amphibian in the world, known scientifically as *Tricho-bactrachus robustus* and to anyone else as the hairy frog.

On a previous visit to the Cameroons, when I had been operating in the lowland forests, my heart had been set on capturing some of these weird creatures, but without success. All the hunters down there to whom I had shown the picture had stoutly denied that any such beast existed. They had looked at me pityingly when I insisted, taking it as just another example of the curiously unbalanced outlook of the white man, for did not everyone know that no frog had hair? Animals had hair, birds had feathers, but frogs had skin and nothing more. Since they didn't believe the creature existed, they didn't bother to search for it, in spite of the huge rewards I offered for its capture. What was the use of looking for a mythical monster, a frog with hair? I had spent many exhausting nights in the forest, wading up and down streams in search of the elusive amphibian, but with no result, and I had come to believe that, in spite of the textbooks, the hunters were right: the creature was not to be found in the lowland forests. I had been so disillusioned by the scorn and derision that any mention of the hairy frog had provoked among the lowland tribes that on my second trip I had not shown the drawing, feeling that the highland hunters would be of the same opinion as their relatives in the great forests. Hence my excitement and astonishment when the young hunter, unprompted, had identified the fabulous beast.

I questioned the hunters closely, quivering like an expectant bloodhound. Yes, for the third time, they did know the beasts; yes, it did have hair; yes, it was easy to catch. When I asked where it was found they made sweeping gestures, indicating that the woods were full of them. With glittering eyes I asked them if they knew of any particular spot. Yes, they knew of a "small water" some two miles away where there were generally a few to be seen at night. That was enough for me. I rushed out on the veranda and uttered a roar. The staff came tumbling out of their hut, bleary-eyed, half asleep, and assembled on the veranda.

"Dis hunter man savvay which side I go find dis frog 'e get beer beer for 'e larse," I explained, "so we go catch um one time."

"*Now*, sah?" asked Ben, horrified.

"Yes, now now, all you go get bag and torch, quickly quickly."

"For nighttime?" asked Ben faintly, for he loved his bed.

"Yes, *now*. Don't just stand there yawning! Go and get torches and bags!"

The reluctant staff, puffy-eyed and yawning, shuffled off to obey. Jacob, the cook, stopped for a moment to explain to me that he was a cook and not a hunter and that he did not see why he should be expected to change his vocation at four o'clock in the morning.

"My friend," I said firmly, "if you no get bag and torch in five minutes, tomorrow you no be hunter man *or* cook, savvay?"

Hastily he followed the rest of the staff in search of frog-hunting equipment. Within half an hour my sleepy band was assembled, and we set off down the dewy road on the hunt for the hairy frogs.

5. THE HUNT FOR THE HAIRY FROGS

In the dim starlight we walked down the dusty road, the grass on either side glistening and heavy with dew. There was no moon, which was most fortunate: when you are hunting at night by torchlight, a moon is a hindrance and not a help, for it casts strange shadows in which your quarry can disappear, and it swamps your torch beam, making it appear so faint that you cannot pick out anything with it.

The little group of hunters walked ahead, wide awake and eager, while my well-paid staff trailed behind, dragging their toes in the dust and yawning prodigiously. Only Jacob, having decided that as the hunt was inevitable he had better make the best of it, walked beside me. Occasionally he would glance over his shoulder with a snort of derision as a more than usually powerful yawn made itself heard from behind. "Dis people no get power," he said scornfully.

"I tink sometime they done forget I go pay five shillings for dis frog we go hunt," I explained loudly and clearly. My voice carried well in the still night air, and immediately the yawning and the dragging footsteps ceased and the rear column became very much awake. Five shillings was a large sum to pay for a frog.

"I no forget," said Jacob slyly, grinning up at me.

"That I don't doubt," I said severely. "You're a thoroughly unprincipled West African Shylock."

"Yes, sah," Jacob agreed unemotionally. It was impossible to crush him: if he did not understand he simply played safe and agreed with everything you said.

We walked down the road for perhaps a mile and a half, and then the hunters turned off onto a narrow path through the long grass, a path that was slippery with dew and that led in an erratic series of zigzags up the side of a hill. All round us in the damp tangle of long grass the tiny frogs and crickets were calling, like a million Lilliputian metronomes; once a large, pale moth spiralled vaguely from the side of the path, and as it fluttered upwards a nightjar came out of the shadows, as swiftly and smoothly as an arrow, and I heard the click of its beak as the moth disappeared. The bird turned and skimmed off down the hillside as silently as it had come.

When we reached the crest of the hill the hunters informed me that the small stream they referred to lay in the valley ahead. It was a deep, narrow, shadow-filled cleft that ran between two smooth buttock-shaped hills, and the curving line of the stream was marked by a dark fringe of small trees and bushes. As we descended into the gloom of the valley the sound of water came to us, gurgling and clopping among the boulders of its bed, and the surface of the path turned to glutinous clay that made

unpleasant sucking noises round our feet as we picked our way
down, slipping and sliding.

The stream fled to the valley, slithering down a series of wide,
shallow, boulder-strewn steps. At the edge of each step was a
diminutive waterfall, perhaps eight feet high, and here the
stream gathered itself into a polished column of water and
plunged down into a circular pool gouged out among the rocks,
where it swirled round and round in a nest of silver bubbles
before diving on among the litter of rocks towards the next
fall. The long grass curved over the edge of the stream in an
uncombed mane of golden hair, and among the glistening boulders grew delicate ferns and tiny plants, embedded in thick
moss that spread everywhere like a layer of green velvet. On
the bank, walking delicately on tiptoe, were numbers of small
pink and chocolate-coloured crabs, and as our torch beams
picked them out they raised their claws menacingly and backed,
with infinite caution, down the holes in the red clay that they
had dug for themselves. Dozens of minute white moths rose
from the long grass and drifted out across the stream like clouds
of snowflakes.

We squatted on the bank to have a smoke and discuss our
plan of campaign. The hunters explained that the best place to
search for frogs was in the pools at the base of the small waterfalls, but that they were also to be found under flat rocks in the
shallower parts of the stream. I decided that we had better
spread out in a line across the stream and wade up it, turning
over every movable stone and searching every nook and cranny
that might harbour a hairy frog. This we did, and for an hour
we worked our way steadily uphill towards the source of the
stream, splashing through the shallow icy water, slipping on

the wet rocks, shining our torches into every hiding place and turning over the loose rocks with infinite care.

There were plenty of crabs, scuttling and clicking among the stones, and bullet-shaped frogs of bright green that leaped into the water with loud plops and startled us. There was a wavering curtain of small moths fluttering everywhere, and small bats flicked in and out of our torch beams, but no hairy frogs. We walked for the most part in silence: there were the hundred different voices of the stream as it moved in its bed, the zinging of crickets in the long grass, the occasional cry of a bird disturbed by our torch beams, the sucking gurgle, followed by a splash, as one of us turned a stone over in deep water. Once, when we were negotiating a small cliff over which, like a pulsating lace curtain, hung a waterfall, we were startled by a loud scream. Directing our battery of lights down to the base of the fall, we found that Jacob, who had been last to scale the cliff, had put his foot on a water snake that lay coiled up in a hollow. In his fright he had attempted to leap in the air, an action that was not very successful, for he was clinging precariously to the cliff face some five feet from the ground. He fell into the pool at the base of the falls and emerged unhurt but soaking wet, his teeth chattering from his immersion in the freezing waters.

The eastern skies were turning slowly from black to pale green with the coming of the dawn, and still we had not found our elusive amphibian. The hunters, who were acutely depressed by our failure, explained that it was useless continuing the search once it was light, for then the frog would not show itself. This meant that we had approximately two hours left in which to track down the beast and capture it. Though we con-

tinued on our way up the stream I was convinced that our luck
was out and that we would not be successful. At last, damp,
cold, and dispirited, we came to a broad, flat valley filled with
great boulders through which the stream picked its way like a
snake. At certain points the stream had formed deep, quiet pools
among the rocks, and as the ground was flat the movement of
the water, which had doubled in width, was slow and even.
The boulders were strewn haphazardly about, all tilted at peculiar angles like giant, archaic gravestones, black under the
starry sky. Each one was tapestried with moss and hung with
sprawling wild begonias.

We had moved about halfway up this valley when I decided
to break off for a cigarette. At the edge of a small pool that lay
like a black mirror ringed round with tall rocks I chose a smooth
dry stone to sit on, switched off my torch, and sat down to enjoy my smoke. The torch beams of my retinue twinkled and
flashed among the rocks as the men continued up the valley,
and the splashing of their feet in the water was soon lost among
the many night sounds. When I had finished I flipped the butt
of my cigarette into the air so that it swooped like a glowing
firefly and fell into the pool, where it extinguished itself with
a hiss. Almost immediately afterwards something jumped into
the pool with a loud plop, and the smooth black waters were disturbed by a thousand silver ripples. I switched on my torch
quickly and shone it on the surface of the water, but there was
nothing to be seen. Then I flashed the beam along the moss-
covered rocks forming the lip of the pool. There, not a yard
from where I was sitting, squatted a gleaming, chocolate-
coloured frog, its fat thighs and the sides of its body covered
with a tangled pelt of something that looked like hair.

I sat there hardly daring to breathe, for the frog was perched on the extreme edge of the rock overhanging the pool; it was alert and suspicious, its legs bunched up ready to jump. If it was frightened, it would leap straight off the rock and into the dark waters, and then there would be no hope of catching it. For perhaps five minutes I remained as immobile as the rocks, and gradually, as it got used to the light, the hairy frog relaxed. Once it shifted its position slightly, blinking its moist eyes, and I was filled with panic, thinking it was going to jump. But it settled down again, and I sighed with relief. As I sat there I was busy working out a plan: first, I had to switch the torch from my right to my left hand without disturbing the creature; then I had to lean forward until my hand was near enough to the fat body to risk grabbing at it. The shifting of the torch caused me acute anguish, for the frog watched the manoeuvre suspiciously. When I had achieved the change I sat quietly for a few minutes to allow it to settle down again, then, with great caution, I moved my cupped hand slowly towards it, inch by inch, until my hand was hanging just above it. I took a deep breath and grabbed. As my hand swooped downwards the frog jumped, but not quite quickly enough, and my grasping fingers caught one slippery hind leg. But the frog was not going to give up its liberty without a fight and uttered a loud screaming gurk; it kicked out frantically with its free hind leg, scraping its toes across the back of my hand. I felt as though my hand had been scratched with several needles, and several deep grooves on the skin turned red with the welling blood. I was so astonished at this unexpected attack from a creature I had thought harmlesss that I must have relaxed my hold slightly. The frog gave an extra hard kick and a wiggle, his moist leg slid through my

HAIRY FROG

fingers, there was a plop as he hit the water, and the ripples danced. My hairy frog had escaped.

My heart, if I might put it like that, was too full for words. An extensive collection of lurid descriptive phrases I had accumulated over the years seemed anaemic and inadequate to describe this catastrophe. I tried one or two, but they were a very weak indication of how I felt. After all this time, after being told that it did not exist, I had come face to face with a hairy frog; after many hours of fruitless search I had actually had the beast in my grasp, and then, through my own stupidity, had let it get away.

I clambered up on a tall rock to see where my hunters had got to. I could see their lights flashing a quarter of a mile away down the valley, and I uttered the prolonged yodelling call the hunters use to communicate with one another. When they answered me I shouted that they were to hurry back, as I had found the beef we were looking for. Then I climbed down and examined the pool carefully. It was perhaps ten feet long and about five feet across at the widest point. It was fed and emptied through two very narrow channels among the rocks, and I decided that if we blocked these, and the frog was still in the pool, we stood a fair chance of recapturing it. When my panting hunters arrived I explained what had happened, and they clicked their fingers and groaned with annoyance.

We set to work and soon had blocked the entrance and exit channels of the pool with piles of flat stones. Then two of the hunters stood on the rocks and shone a battery of torches into the pool, so that we could see what we were doing. First, I tested the depths of the water with the long handle of the butterfly net. It was about two feet deep; the bottom of the pool was of coarse gravel and small stones, a terrain that provided ample hiding places for the frog. Jacob, two hunters, and I removed all the garments we had on and slid into the icy water: Jacob and I at one end of the pool, the two hunters at the other. Slowly we moved towards each other, bent double, feeling with our fingers and toes in every crack, turning over every stone. We were near the centre of the pool when one of the hunters gave a yelp of delight and grabbed wildly at something under the water, almost losing his balance and falling on his face.

"Na whatee, na whatee?" everyone chorused excitedly.

"Na flog," spluttered the hunter, "but 'e done run."

"You no get hand?" inquired Jacob wrathfully through chattering teeth.

" 'E done run for Masa," said the hunter, pointing in my direction.

As he spoke I felt something moving near my bare feet and I bent down and groped frantically under the water. At the same moment Jacob uttered a shrill scream and dived under the water. One of the hunters also clutched at something between his legs. My hand felt a smooth, fat body burrowing in the gravel near my toes, and I grabbed at it. Jacob reappeared above the water, spitting and gasping and waving one arm triumphantly, his hand clasped firmly round a fat frog. He splashed through the water towards me to show me his capture, and as he reached me I straightened up with my own prize caught in my cupped hands. I glanced hurriedly between my fingers and had a quick glimpse of the frog's thick thighs covered with a mat of the hairlike substance: it was a hairy frog. Then I looked at Jacob's capture: he had caught one too. After congratulating each other we cautiously placed our frogs in a deep, soft cloth bag, and tied up the mouth of it carefully. We had just finished when the hunter who had been groping wildly between his legs straightened up with a roar of delight, swinging yet another hairy frog by the leg.

Warmed and encouraged by our success, we plunged back into the pool and searched it carefully, but we found no more frogs. By now the rim of the eastern horizon was a pale powder blue, flecked with gold, and in the sky above us the remaining stars were flickering and dying as stripes of jade green spread across the sky. It was obviously too late to continue our hunt, but I was well pleased with the results. As the Africans crouched on the rocks, laughing and chattering, smoking the cigarettes I had distributed, I dried myself, rather inadequately, with my handkerchief and put on my dew-soaked clothes. My head was aching savagely, partly, I think, from the excitement of the capture, but principally from the Fon's party. However, with the glow of triumph enveloping me, I cared not for the cold dampness of my clothes nor for my aching head. The bag with the hairy frogs inside I dipped into the pool until it was sodden and cool, then I wrapped it in wet grass and placed it in the bottom of the basket.

As we reached the top of the hill the sun rose above the distant mountains and flooded the world with a brittle, golden light. The long grass was bent and heavy with dampness, and a thousand tiny spiders had spun their nets among the stalks, and the nets had dredged up from the night a rich haul of dewdrops that shone white and ice-blue in the sun. Dozens of great locusts leaped up from under our feet and sped over the grass in a whirring glitter of magenta-coloured wings; and some fat bumblebees, electric blue and as furry as bears, formed a

BUMBLEBEES AND ORCHIDS

humming choir over a group of pale yellow orchids growing in the shelter of a large rock. The air was fresh and cool, full of the scent of flowers, grass, earth, and dew. The hunters, happy in the knowledge that the night's activities had been successful, broke into song as they picked their way down the path in single file: a lilting Bafutian melody rendered with great verve. The staff joined in, and Jacob beat a gentle tattoo on a collecting tin by way of accompaniment. Thus we marched back to Bafut, singing loudly, Jacob working out more and more complicated rhythms on his improvised drum.

My first job, when we at last reached home, was to house the frogs. I filled a deep tin with fresh water, placed a number of stones at the bottom to act as cover, and put two of the frogs into it. The third I placed in a large jam jar. While I had my

HAIRY FROG

breakfast the jam jar rested on the table, and between mouth-
fuls I contemplated my capture with adoring eyes.

My hairy frog was, as frogs go, quite large: with its legs
tucked neatly in, it would have fitted on a saucer without very
much room left over. The head was broad and rather flat, with

protuberant eyes and an extraordinarily wide, gaping mouth. The ground colour of the upper parts was a deep chocolate brown, mottled dimly in places with darker brown, almost black, markings; the underside was white, flushed with pink on the lower belly and the inside of the thighs. The eyes were very large, jet black netted with a fine filigree of golden marks. The most astonishing thing about the creature—the hair—was confined to the sides of the body and the thighs, where it grew thick and black, about a quarter of an inch long. This adornment is not really hair at all but fine, elongated filaments of skin, which, on close examination, resemble the tentacles of a sea anemone. Until you examine the creature closely, however, the illusion that its hindquarters are clothed in a thick layer of fur is complete. In the water the hair stands out, floating like weed, and so is seen to the best advantage; when the frog is out of water the hair takes on a tangled, jellylike look.

There has been much controversy, ever since this frog was first discovered, over the exact use of this curious hirsute decoration, but it is now believed that the filaments act as an aid to respiration. All frogs breathe, to a certain extent, through their skins; that is to say, the skin absorbs oxygen from the moisture around it. In this way a frog has, so to speak, two breathing apparatuses, the skin and the lungs. By breathing through the skin a frog can stay submerged in the water for quite considerable periods. In the case of the hairy frog, the great numbers of filaments give it a considerably increased skin area, and so must aid its respiration a good deal. Originally, because only the male is hairy—the female is smooth-skinned like any ordinary frog—the hairs were thought to be purely ornamental rather than useful, for it seemed ridiculous to suppose that the male was so short-winded that he needed hair to enable him to breathe properly, while the female pursued a hairless and well-aerated existence. However, this unusual discrepancy was soon explained: it was found that the male spends much of his life submerged in water, whereas the female leads a purely terrestrial existence, going to water only during the mating season. So the mystery was explained: the female, on land, uses the lungs to breathe with for the most part, whereas her husband finds the hairs a very useful addition in his watery lair.

Next to its hairiness the most curious thing about this frog is that it possesses, in the fleshy toes of each hind foot, a set of long, semitransparent white claws, which, like those of a cat, are retractile and when not in use disappear into sheaths in the toes. That these claws are sharp and useful had been proved to me by the scratches on the back of my hand. I should imagine that the use of these weapons is twofold: first, as a means of defence, and, second, as a useful tool, enabling the amphibian to cling to the slippery rocks in the fast-running streams it inhabits. Whenever the frogs were picked up they would kick out frantically with their hind legs and the claws would appear from their sheaths; at the same time they would utter their curious screaming grunts, a cross between a contented pig and a tortured mouse, a sound astonishingly loud and inclined to be very startling when you were not expecting it.

My hairy frogs settled down very nicely in their large tin, and eventually, after numerous night hunts, I added to their number until I had seven, all males with the most luxuriant backsides. For many weeks I searched high and low for some females to go with them, but without success. Then, one day,

a dear old lady who looked about ninety-five appeared on the
veranda with two calabashes: in one was a pair of shrews, and
in the other was a large female hairy frog. This was the only
female of the species I ever obtained, and so she was given
special care and attention. She was similar to the males in appearance, except that her skin was dryer and slightly rougher,
and her colouring was a bright brick-red with chocolate-
coloured flecks. She settled down quite happily with her seven
suitors, and even adopted their habits: during the day they all
lay in the water, almost completely submerged, ready to dive
to the bottom of the tin should anyone approach; at night,
however, they grew braver, and climbed out on the rocks I had
put in there for them, where they would sit gulping at each
other with vacant expressions. During all the time I had them
in Africa, and on the long voyage back to England, the frogs
stubbornly refused to eat any of the tempting delicacies I put
before them. But they were extremely fat, and so this long fast
did not worry me unduly, for most reptiles can go for long
periods without food and be none the worse for it.

When the time came for me to leave Bafut and travel down
to the base camp, and then on to the coast, I packed the frogs
in a shallow wooden box filled with wet banana leaves. The
box had to be shallow, otherwise the frogs, when scared, would
jump wildly into the air and bang their delicate noses on the
wooden top; in a shallow box they had no chance to do this.
They caused me considerable trouble on the way down from
Bafut, and many anxious moments: in the highlands the climate
is cool and pleasant, but as you descend into the forested lowlands it's like entering a Turkish bath, and the frogs did not
enjoy this change. When I opened the box, during one of our

halts on the way down, I was horrified to find all my hairy frogs lying in the bottom, limp and apparently lifeless. I rushed frantically down into a nearby ravine and plunged the box into a stream. Gradually the cool waters revived four of them, but three were too far gone and soon died. This left me with three males and the female. I had to stop the lorry every two or three miles for the rest of the journey, while I ducked the frog box into a stream to revive its inmates, and it was only in this fashion that I managed to get them to base camp alive.

On arrival, however, I discovered another problem: the hairy frogs had not been able to jump and damage their noses, but they had tried to burrow into the corners of the box and had managed to rub off all the skin on their noses and upper lips. This was most serious, for once the delicate skin on a frog's nose is damaged, it very soon develops a nasty sore on the spot, which spreads like a rodent ulcer and can, eventually, eat away the whole nose and lip. Hastily I had to create a new box for the frogs to live in. This one was also shallow, but it was completely padded inside, top, bottom, and sides, with soft cloth stuffed with cotton wool. In this small padded cell the hairy frogs did very well; whether they jumped or burrowed, they could not damage themselves on the soft surface. By keeping them drier than usual I managed to heal their scraped noses, but they retained faint white scars.

When we finally left the base camp and travelled down to the coast to catch the ship, the journey was a nightmare. It was incredibly hot, and the hairy frogs' box dried up rapidly. I tried keeping it in a tin full of water, but the roads were so bad that most of the water sloshed out inside the first half-mile. The only alternative was to stop the lorry at a stream every half-hour or so and give the box a thorough soaking. In spite of this, one of the males succumbed, and so only three hairy frogs arrived on board ship. The cool sea breeze soon revived them, and they seemed fit enough, though very thin. Their self-imposed fast continued until they reached England, and for some time after they were installed in the Reptile House at the London Zoo. The curator tried to tempt them with all sorts of delicious tidbits, as I had done, but they still refused to eat. Then, one day, more or less as a last resort, he put some pink, newly born white mice into their cage, and, to his surprise, the frogs fell on them and devoured the lot as though baby mice were their favourite food. From then on they lived entirely on this mammalian diet, refusing all the usual froggy foods like locusts and mealworms. It seems highly improbable that they live exclusively on baby mice in the wild state, so it must be that the mice resembled the food that they were used to eating, though what that is remains shrouded in mystery.

6.　　　　SNAKES AND SHILLINGS

The Fon's speech at the grass-gathering ceremony produced
astonishing and immediate results. The next afternoon, in an
endeavour to dissipate the effects of the Fon's party and the
subsequent frog hunt, I lay down for a couple of hours to catch
up on some sleep. When I awoke I decided that tea might help
restore me to a more amiable frame of mind, and I staggered off
the bed and made my way to the door, intending to shout my
instructions down to the kitchen from the veranda. I opened
the door and then stopped dead, wondering if I was dreaming,
for the whole veranda was literally covered with a weird assortment of sacks, palm-leaf baskets, and calabashes, all of
which shook and quivered gently. Leaning up against the wall
were four or five long bamboos to the ends of which were tied

writhing, infuriated snakes. The veranda looked like a native market.

At the top of the steps squatted Jacob, scowling at me disapprovingly. "Masa wake up?" he said mournfully. "Why Masa wake up?"

"What's all this?" I asked, waving my hand at the collection of bags and baskets.

"Beef," said Jacob succinctly.

I examined the snakes' bonds to make sure they were secure. "Which man done bring dis beef?" I asked, feeling rather stunned by the profusion of the arrivals.

"Dis men done bring um," said Jacob laconically, gesturing down the steps behind him.

I stepped over to where he sat and saw that the seventy-five steps up to the villa, and a good deal of the road beyond, were jammed with Bafutians of all ages and sexes. There must have been about a hundred and fifty of them, and they gazed up at me, unmoving and strangely quiet. As a rule a small group of four or five Africans can make more noise than any other people on earth, yet this great crowd might have been composed of deaf mutes for all the sound it was making. The silence was uncanny.

"What's the matter with them?" I asked Jacob.

"Sah?"

"Why dey no make noise, eh?"

"Ah," said Jacob, light dawning, "I done tell um Masa 'e sleep."

This was the first of many examples I was to have of the courtesy and good manners of the Bafut people. For nearly two hours, I discovered, they had sat there in the hot sun, curbing their natural exuberance so that my slumbers might not be disturbed.

"Why you no wake me before?" I said to Jacob. "You no savvay na bad ting for dis beef to wait, eh?"

"Yes, sah. Sorry, sah."

"All right. Let's get on with it and see what they've brought."

I picked up the first basket and peered into it: it contained five mice with pale ginger fur, white bellies, and long tails. I handed the basket to Jacob, who carried it to the top of the steps and held it aloft. "Who done bring dis beef?" he shouted.

"I done bring um," called an old woman. She fought her way up onto the veranda, bargained with me breathlessly for five minutes, then fought her way down the steps again, clutching her money.

The next basket contained two delightful little owls. They were speckled grey and black, and the area round the eyes was pure white with a black rim, so that they looked as though they were wearing large horn-rimmed glasses. They clicked their beaks at me and lowered their long eyelashes over their fierce golden eyes when they saw me, and as I tried to pick them up they rolled over on their backs, presenting their large talons and uttering loud screams. They were quite young, and in places were still clad in the cottony down of infancy, so that they looked as if they had both been caught in a snowstorm. I can never resist owls at the best of times, and these two babies were quite adorable. They were white-faced Scops owls, and something quite new to my collection, so I had an excellent reason for buying them.

The next item was a squirrel, who created considerable diversion. As soon as I opened the palm-leaf bag he shot out like

OWLETS

a Jack-in-the-box, bit my hand, and galloped off across the veranda. Jacob gave chase, and as he drew near the squirrel suddenly darted to one side and then ran down the steps, weaving skilfully through the dozens of black legs that stood there. The panic created was tremendous: those on the first step leaped into the air, lost their balance, and fell backwards against those on the next step. They, in turn, fell against the ones below them, who went down like grass before a scythe. In a matter of seconds the steps were covered with a tangled mass of struggling bodies, with arms and legs sticking out at the oddest angles. I quite thought that the unfortunate squirrel would be crushed to death under this human avalanche, but to my surprise he appeared at the bottom of the steps apparently unhurt, flipped his tail a couple of times, and set off down the road at a brisk trot.

At the top of the steps I was fuming impotently and struggling to push my way down through the tangle of Africans, for

the squirrel was a rarity, and I was determined that he should
not escape. Halfway down someone clutched my ankle, and I
sat down abruptly on top of a large body, which, judging from
the bits I could see, was female. I glanced desperately down at
the road as I endeavoured to regain my feet, and to my joy I
saw a band of some twenty young men approaching. They saw
the squirrel and stopped short, and the squirrel sat up and
sniffed at them suspiciously.

"You!" I roared. "You dere for de road! Catch dat beef!"

The young men put down their bundles and advanced determinedly upon the squirrel, who took one look at them,
turned, and fled. They set off in hot pursuit, each determined
that he should be the one to recapture the rodent. The squirrel
ran well, but he was no match for the long legs of his pursuers.
In a tight bunch they drew level, their faces grim and set. Then,
to my horror, they launched themselves at my precious specimen in a body, and for the second time the squirrel disappeared
under a huge pile of struggling Africans. This time, I thought,
the poor beast really would be crushed, but that squirrel seemed
indestructible. When the heap in the road had sorted itself out
a bit, one of the young men was holding the chattering and
panting squirrel by the scruff of its neck.

"Masa!" he called, "I done catch um!"

I threw down a bag for him to put the animal in, and then
it was passed up the steps to me. Hastily I got the beast into a
cage, so that I could make sure he was not damaged in any way.
He seemed all right, except for the fact that he was in an extremely bad temper. He was a black-eared squirrel, perhaps one
of the most beautiful of the Cameroon squirrels. The upper
parts were a deep olive green, while the belly was a rich yellow-

orange. Along the sides were a series of white spots, set in a line from shoulder to buttocks, and there was a rim of black fur marking the edge of each ear, making him look as though he had never washed behind them. But the most beautiful part of the furry anatomy was the tail. This was long and tremendously bushy; the upper parts were a brindled greeny-brown, while the underparts were the most vivid flame-orange imaginable. In the cage the squirrel flipped his dazzling tail at me once or twice, then squatted down to the stern task of devouring a mango I had put in there. I watched him fondly, thinking what a lucky escape he had had, and how pleased I was to have got him. If I had known what trouble he was going to cause in the future I might have viewed his arrival with considerably less excitement.

I turned my attention back to the various containers littering the veranda and picked up a large calabash at random. As usual, the neck was stuffed with a tightly packed plug of green leaves. I removed these and peered into the depths, but the calabash was so capacious and so dark I could not see what was inside. I carried it to the head of the steps and held it up.

"Which side de man who done bring dis calabash?" I asked.

"Na me, sah, na me!" shouted a man halfway down the steps.

It was always a source of astonishment to me how the Africans could distinguish their own calabashes out of hundreds of others. Except for a difference in size, I could never tell one from the other, but the Africans knew at a glance which was theirs and which belonged to some other hunter.

"What beef 'e dere dere for inside?" I asked, negligently swinging the calabash by its cord.

"Snake, sah," said the man.

I hastily replaced the plug of green leaves. "What kind of snake, my friend?"

"Na gera, sah."

I consulted my list of local names and found this meant a green-leaf viper. These were common and beautiful snakes in Bafut, and I already had quite a number of them. They were about eighteen inches long, a startlingly bright grass green in colour, with canary-yellow bellies and broad diagonal white stripes along their sides. I carried the calabash over to empty the new arrival into the shallow, gauze-topped box in which I kept the vipers.

Emptying a snake from a calabash into a cage is one of the simplest of operations, providing you observe one or two rudimentary rules. First, make sure that any inmates of the cage are far away from the door. This I did. Second, make sure how many snakes you have in the calabash before starting to shake them out. This I omitted to do.

I opened the door of the cage, unplugged the mouth of the calabash, and began to shake gently. Sometimes it requires quite a lot of shaking to get a snake out of a calabash, for it will coil itself inside and press against the sides. Jacob stood behind me, breathing heavily down my neck, and behind him stood a solid wall of Africans, watching open-mouthed. I shook the calabash gently, and nothing happened. I shook it a bit harder, with the same result. I had never known a viper to cling with such tenacity to the interior of a receptacle. Becoming irritated, I gave the calabash a really vigorous shake, and it promptly broke in half. An intricately tangled knot of green-leaf vipers, composed of about half a dozen large, vigorous, and angry snakes, fell out on the cage with what can be described only as a sickening thud.

They were plaited together in such a large, solid ball that
instead of falling through the door and into the cage they got
jammed halfway, so that I could not slam the door on them.
Then, with a fluid grace I had no time to admire, they disen-
tangled themselves and wriggled determinedly over the edge
of the door and onto the floor, where they spread out fanwise,
with almost military precision. Jacob, and the Africans who had
been jammed behind him, disappeared with the startling sud-
denness of a conjuring trick. I could hardly blame them, for
none of them was wearing shoes. But I was not dressed for
gallivanting with a tribe of vipers either, for I was wearing
shorts and a pair of sandals. My only armament, moreover, consisted of the two halves of the broken calabash, which is not the
most useful thing to have when tackling a snake. Leaving the
snakes in sole charge of the veranda, I shot into my bedroom,
found a stick, and went cautiously out again. The snakes had
scattered widely, and so they were quite easy to corner, pin
down with the stick, and pick up. One by one I dropped them
into the cage and, with a sigh of relief, shut and locked the door.
The Africans reappeared just as suddenly as they had disappeared, all chattering and laughing and clicking their fingers as
they described to one another the great danger they had been
in.

I fixed the snake bringer with a very cold eye. "You!" I said.
"Why you no tell me dere be plenty snake for inside dat calabash, eh?"

"Whah!" he said, looking surprised. "I done tell Masa dere
be snake for inside."

"Snake, yes. *One* snake. You no tell me dere be six for inside."

"I done tell Masa dere be snake for inside," he repeated indignantly.

"I done ask you what beef you done bring," I explained patiently, "and you say 'snake.' You no say dere be six snake. How you tink I go savvay how many snake you bring, eh? You tink sometime I get juju for my eye and I go savvay how many snake you done catch?"

"Stupid man," said Jacob, joining in the fray, "sometime dis snake bite Masa, and Masa go die. Den how you go do, eh?"

I turned on Jacob. "I noticed that you were conspicuous by your absence, my noble and heroic creature."

"Yes, sah!" said Jacob, beaming.

It was quite late in the evening before the last hunter had been paid, and I was left with such a weird assortment of live creatures on my hands that it took me until three o'clock the following morning to cage them. Even so, there were five large rats left over, and no box from which to make a cage. I was forced to release them in my bedroom, where, for some obscure reason, they spent the entire night trying to gnaw through the leg of the table.

The next morning I cleaned out and fed my now considerable collection. I didn't expect anything more to turn up that day— but I was wrong. The Bafutians had thrown themselves wholeheartedly into the task of providing me with specimens, and by ten o'clock the roadway and the seventy-five steps were black with people, and in desperation I had to bargain for the creatures. By lunchtime it was obvious that the supply of animals had far exceeded my store of wood and boxes to make cages for them, and I was forced to employ a team of small boys to tour Bafut and buy up any and every box or plank of wood they could find. The prices I had to pay were exorbitant, for to the African any sort of receptacle, be it a bottle, an old tin, or a box, is worth its weight in gold.

By four o'clock both the staff and I were exhausted, and we had been bitten so many times in so many places by such a variety of creatures that any additional bites went almost unnoticed. The whole villa was overflowing with animals, and they squeaked and chirruped, rattled and bumped, in their calabashes, baskets, and sacks, while we worked furiously to make the cages. It was one of those days one prefers to forget. By midnight we were all so tired we could hardly keep awake, and there were still some ten cages to be made. A large pot of tea, heavily laced with whisky, gave us a sort of spurious enthusiasm for our task and carried us on. At two-thirty the last nail was driven in and the last animal released in its new quarters. As I crawled into bed I was horribly aware of the fact that I should have to be up at six the next morning if I wanted to have everything cleaned and fed by the time the next influx of specimens began.

The next day was, if anything, slightly worse than the preceding one, for the Bafutians started to arrive before I had finished attending to the collection. There is nothing quite so nerve-racking as struggling to clean and feed several dozen creatures when twenty or thirty more have arrived in airless, insanitary containers and are crying out for attention. As I watched, out of the corners of my eyes, the pile of calabashes and baskets growing on the veranda, so the number of cages that I had still to attend to seemed to multiply, until I felt rather as Hercules must have felt when he got his first glimpse of the Augean stables.

Before buying any fresh specimens I made a speech to the assembled Bafutians from the top of the steps. I pointed out that in the last couple of days they had brought me a vast quantity of beef of all shapes, sizes, and descriptions. This proved that the Bafutians were by far the best hunters I had come across, and I was very grateful to them. However, I went on, as they would realize, there was a limit to the amount of beef I could purchase and house in any one day. So I would be glad if they would desist from hunting for the space of three days, in order that my caging and food supply might catch up with them. There was no sense, I pointed out, in my buying beef if it was going to die for lack of adequate housing; that was just simply a waste of money. The African is nothing if not a businessman, and at this remark the nodding of heads sent a ripple over the crowd, and a chorus of "arrrrr!" arose. Having driven the point home, and, I hoped, given myself three days' respite, I purchased the animals and once more set about the task of cage building.

At four o'clock the caging was under control, and I was having a break for a cup of tea. Leaning on the veranda rail, I saw the arched doorway in the red brick wall fly open, and the Fon appeared. He strode across the great courtyard, his robes fluttering and hissing as he moved. He was scowling worriedly and muttering to himself. As it was obvious that he was on his way to pay me a visit I went down the steps to meet him.

"Iseeya, my friend," I said politely.

"My friend," he said, enveloping my hand in his and peering earnestly into my face, "some man done tell me you no go buy beef again. Na so?"

"No be so," I said.

"Ah! Good, good!" he said, relieved. "Sometime I fear you done get enough beef an' you go lef' dis place."

"No, no be so," I explained. "People for Bafut savvay hunting too much, and dey done bring me so many beef I no get box for put um. So I done tell all dis people dey no go hunt for three days, so I get chance for make box for put all dis beef."

"Ah! I savvay," said the Fon, smiling at me affectionately. "I tink sometime you go lef' us."

"No, I no go lef' Bafut."

The Fon peered anxiously round in a conspiratorial fashion, and then, draping one arm lovingly round my shoulders, he drew me down the road. "My friend," he said in a hoarse whisper, "I done find beef for you. Na foine beef, na beef you never get."

"What kind of beef?" I asked curiously.

"Beef," said the Fon explicitly, "you go like too much. We go catch um now, eh?"

"You never catch um yet?"

"No, my friend, but I savvay which side dey de hide."

"All right. We go look um now, eh?"

"Yes, yes, foine!" said the Fon.

Eagerly he led me across the courtyard, through a maze of narrow passages, until we reached a small hut. "Wait here small time, my friend, I go come," he said and disappeared into the hut's gloomy interior.

I waited outside, wondering where he had gone to and what kind of beef it was that he had discovered. The air of mystery about him made the whole thing rather intriguing.

When he reappeared, for a moment I did not recognize him. He had removed his robes, his skullcap, and his sandals and was

naked except for a small, spotlessly white loincloth. In one hand
he held a long, slender spear. His thin, muscular body gleamed
with oil, and his feet were bare. He approached me, twirling his
spear professionally, beaming with delight at my obvious surprise.

"You done get new hunter man," he said, chuckling. "Now
you fit call me Bafut Beagle, no be so?"

"I tink dis hunter man be best for all," I said, grinning.

"I savvay hunting fine," he said, nodding. "Sometime my
people tink I get ole too much for go bush. My friend, if some
man get hunting for 'e eye, for 'e nose, an' for 'e blood, 'e *never*
get ole too much for go bush, no be so?"

"You speak true, my friend," I said.

He led me out of the environs of his compound, along the
road for perhaps half a mile, and then branched off through
some maize fields. He walked at a great pace, twirling his spear
and humming to himself, occasionally turning to grin at me.
Mischievous delight illuminated his features.

We left the fields, passed through a small thicket of mimbo
palms, dark and mysterious and full of the rustling of the fronds,
and started to climb up the golden hillside. At the top the Fon
paused, stuck his spear into the ground, folded his arms, and
surveyed the view. I had stopped a little way down the hillside
to collect some small delicately coloured snails. When I reached
the top the Fon appeared to have gone into a trance.

Presently he sighed deeply, and, turning towards me, he
smiled and swept his arms wide. "Na my country dis," he said.
"Na foine dis country."

I nodded in agreement, and we stood there in silence for a
few minutes and looked at the view.

Below us lay a mosaic of small fields, green and silver and fawn, broken up by small mimbo-palm thickets and an occasional patch of rust red where the earth of a field had been newly hoed. This small area of cultivation was like a coloured handkerchief laid on the earth and forgotten, surrounded on all sides by the great ocean of mountains, their crests gilded and their valleys smudged with shadow by the falling sun. The Fon gazed slowly round, an expression of mixed affection and childlike pleasure on his face. He sighed again, a sigh of satisfaction. "Foine!" he murmured. Then he plucked his spear from the earth and led the way down into the next valley, humming tunefully to himself.

The valley was shallow and flat, thickly overgrown with a wood of small stunted trees, some only about ten feet high. Many were completely invisible under immense cloaks of convolvulus, squat towers of trembling leaves and ivory-coloured flowers. The valley had captured the sunshine of the day, and the warm air was heavy and sweet with the scent of flowers and leaves. A small anonymous bird let a melodious trickle of song fill the valley, then stopped suddenly, so that the only sound was the blurred singing of the bees as they hovered round the trees or waddled up the smooth tunnels of the convolvulus flowers.

The Fon surveyed the trees for a moment before moving quietly through the grass to a better vantage point, where our view into the wood was not so clogged with convolvulus. "Na for here we go see beef," he whispered, pointing at the trees. "We sit down an' wait small time." He squatted down on his haunches and waited with a relaxed immobility.

I squatted down beside him and divided my attention equally

between watching him and watching the trees. As the trees remained devoid of life, I concentrated on my companion, who sat there clutching his spear upright in his large hands.

When he had appeared out of that dark little hut in Bafut, it seemed as though he had not only left behind his robes and trappings of state, but also had shed that regal air which had seemed so much part of his character. Here, crouching in this quiet warm valley, he appeared to be just another hunter, his bright dark eyes fixed on the trees, waiting for the quarry he knew would come. But, as I looked at him, I realized that he was not just another hunter; there was something different about him. Any ordinary hunter would not have crouched there, patient, a trifle bored, for he would have done the same thing so many times before. But the Fon waited, his eyes gleaming, a half-smile on his wide mouth, and I realized that he was thoroughly enjoying himself. I wondered how many times in the past he had become tired of his deferential councillors and his worshipping subjects, and felt his magnificent robes to be hot and cumbersome, and his pointed shoes cramping and hard. Then perhaps the urge had come to him to feel the soft red earth under his bare feet and the wind on his naked body, and so he would steal off to his hut, put on the clothes of a hunter, and stride away over the hills, twirling his spear and humming, pausing on the hilltops to admire the beautiful country over which he ruled.

I remembered the words he had spoken to me only a short time before: "If a man has hunting for his eyes, his nose, and his blood, he never gets too old to go to bush." The Fon, I decided, was definitely that sort of man. My meditations on the Fon's character were abruptly interrupted: he leaned forward and gripped my arm, pointing a long finger at the trees. "Dey done come," he whispered, his face wreathed in smiles.

I followed the pointing of his finger, and for a moment I could see nothing but a confused net of branches. Then something moved, and I saw the animal we had been awaiting.

He came drifting through the tangled branches with all the gentle, airy grace of a piece of thistledown. When he got nearer I discovered that he looked exactly like my idea of a leprechaun: he was clad in a little fur coat of greenish-grey and had a long slender furry tail. The hands, which were pink, were large for his size; the fingers long and attenuated. The ears were large and the skin so fine that it was semitransparent. The ears seemed to have a life of their own, for they twisted and turned independently, crumpling and folding flat to the head as if they were fans, or standing up pricked and straight like anaemic arum lilies. The face of the little creature was dominated by a pair of tremendous dark eyes, eyes that would have put any self-respecting owl to shame. Moreover, the creature could twist his head round and look over his back in much the same way that an owl does. He ran to the tip of a slender branch, which scarcely dipped beneath his weight, and there he sat, clutching the bark with long slender fingers, peering about with his great eyes, and chirruping quietly to himself. This was, I knew, a galago, but he looked much more like something out of a fairy tale.

He sat on the branch, twittering vaguely to himself, for about a minute; then an astonishing thing happened. Quite suddenly the trees were full of galagos, galagos of every age and size, ranging from ones little bigger than a walnut to fully adult ones that could have been quite comfortable in an ordinary drinking glass. They jumped from branch to branch, grasping the leaves and twigs with their large thin hands, twittering softly, and gazing round them with the wide-eyed innocence of a troupe of cherubim. The baby ones, who seemed to be all eyes, kept fairly close to their parents; occasionally they would sit up on their hind legs and hold their tiny pink hands up, fingers spread wide, as though in horror at the depravity they were seeing in the world of leaves around them.

One baby discovered, while I watched, that he was sitting on the same branch as a succulent locust. It was evening time, and the insect was drowsy and slow to realize its danger. Before it could do anything, the baby galago had flitted down the branch and grabbed it firmly round the middle. The locust woke up abruptly and decided that something must be done. It was a large insect, almost as big as the baby galago, in fact, and with its long, muscular hind legs it started to kick out vigorously. The fight was fascinating to watch: the galago clasped the locust desperately in his long fingers and tried to bite, and at each attempt the locust would give a terrific kick and knock its adversary off balance. The galago would fall off the branch and hang beneath, suspended by his feet. When this had happened several times I decided that the galago must have adhesive soles. Even while hanging upside down and being kicked in the stomach by a large locust the galago maintained his expression of wide-eyed innocence. The end of the fight was unexpected: when they were hanging upside down the locust gave an extra-hefty kick, and the galago's feet lost their grip, so both fell through the leaves, clasped together. As they tumbled earthwards the galago loosened one hand from round the locust's waist and grabbed a passing branch with the effortless

GALAGO AND LOCUST

ease of a trained acrobat. He hauled himself onto the branch
and bit the locust's head off before the insect could recover
sufficiently to continue the fight. Holding the decapitated but
still kicking body in one hand, the galago stuffed the insect's
head into his mouth and chewed it with evident enjoyment.
Then he sat, with his head on one side, contemplating the
twitching body in one hand and giving vent to excited screams
of delight. When the corpse had ceased to move and the big
hind legs had stiffened in death, the galago tore them off, one
by one, and ate them. He looked ridiculously like a diminutive elderly gourmet clasping the drumstick of some gigantic
chicken.

Soon the valley was filled with shadow, and it became difficult to see the galagos among the leaves, though we could hear
their soft chittering. We rose from our cramped positions and
made our way back up the hillside. At the top the Fon paused
and gazed down at the woods below, smiling delightedly. "Dat
beef!" he said, chuckling. "I like um too much. All time 'e
make funny for me, an' I go laugh."

"Na fine beef," I said. "How you call um?"

"For Bafut," said the Fon, "we call um shilling."

"You think sometimes my hunter men fit catch some?"

"Tomorrow you go have some," promised the Fon, but he
would not tell me how they were to be captured, nor who was
to do the capturing.

We reached Bafut in the dusk, and when the Fon was re-
spectably clothed once more he came and had a drink. As I
said good night to him I reminded him of his promise.

"Yes, my friend, I no go forget," he said. "I go get you some
shilling."

Four days passed, and I began to think that either the Fon had forgotten or else the creatures were proving more difficult to capture than he had imagined. Then, on the fifth morning, my tea was brought in, and reposing on the tray was a small, highly coloured raffia basket. I pulled off the lid and looked sleepily inside, and four pairs of enormous, liquid, innocent eyes peered up at me with expressions of gentle inquiry.

It was a basketful of shillings from the Fon.

7.

THE QUE-FONG-GOO

The grassland country was populated by a rich variety of reptile life, and most of it seemed easy to catch. In the lowland forests you very rarely saw a snake of any description, even if you searched carefully. There were snakes there, of course, but I think they were more widely dispersed, and probably the majority of the species were tree dwellers, which made them much more difficult to see and to capture. In the mountains, however, the grass was alive with small rodents and frogs, and the patches of mountain forest filled with birds, and so it was a paradise for snakes. There were great black spitting cobras, green mambas, slim tree snakes with enormous, innocent-looking eyes, the multicoloured Gaboon viper with a forked rhino-like horn on its nose, and a host of others.

There were plenty of frogs and toads, as well as snakes. The frogs ranged in size from the hairy frog down to tiny tree frogs the size of an acorn, some spotted and streaked with such a dazzling array of colours that they looked more like delicious sweets than amphibians. The toads, on the whole, were fairly drab, but they made up for this by being decorated with strange clusters of warts and protuberances on their bodies, and an astonishing variety of colouring in their eyes. But the commonest of the reptiles were the lizards, which could be found everywhere. In the long herbage at the roadside scuttled fat skinks with stubby legs, fawn and silver and black in colour, and on the walls of the huts, in the road, and on the rocks the rainbow-coloured agamas pranced and nodded. Under the bark of trees or beneath stones you could find small geckos with great golden eyes, their bodies neatly and handsomely marked in chocolate and cream, and in the houses at night the ordinary house geckos, translucent and ghostly as pink pearls, paraded across the ceiling.

All these reptiles were brought in to me at one time or another by the local population. Sometimes it would be a snake tied insecurely to the end of a stick or a calabash full of gulping frogs. Sometimes the capture was carefully wrapped in the hunter's hat or shirt or dangled on the end of a fine string. By these haphazard and dangerous methods such things as cobras, mambas, and Gaboon vipers were brought to me, and although their capturers knew their deadliness they were handled with offhand carelessness. As a rule, the African is no fool over snakes and prefers to regard every species as poisonous, just to be on the safe side, so to find the Bafutians treating them with such casualness was surprising. I found it even more surprising when I discovered that the one reptile they all feared intensely was completely harmless.

I was out with the Bafut Beagles one day, and during the course of the hunt we came to a wide, grassy valley about half a mile from the village. The Beagles had wandered off to set the nets, and while waiting for them I sat down in the grass to enjoy a cigarette. Suddenly my attention was attracted by a slight movement to my left, and on looking down I saw a reptile whose appearance made me gasp. Hitherto I had been under the impression that the most colourful lizard in the grassland was the agama, but in comparison to the one that had crawled into view among the grass stems the agama was as dull and colourless as a lump of putty. I sat there hardly daring to move, in case this wonderful creature dashed off into the herbage. As I remained quite still, it eventually decided that I was harmless and slowly and luxuriously slithered out into the sun and lay there contemplating me with its golden-flecked eyes. I could see it was a skink of sorts, but one of the largest and most colourful I had ever seen. It lay there quietly, basking in the early morning sun, and I had plenty of time to examine it. Including its tail, it was about a foot in length and some two inches across the widest part of its body. It had a short, broad head and small but powerful legs. Its colouring and pattern were so dazzling and so intricate that it is almost impossible to describe. To begin with, the scales were large and very slightly raised, so the whole creature looked as though it had been cleverly constructed out of mosaic. The throat was banded lengthwise with black and white, the top of the head was reddish-rust, while the cheeks, upper lip, and chin were bright brick-red. The main body colour was a deep glossy black, against which the other colours showed up extremely well. Running from the angle of the jaw to the front legs were stripes of bright cherry red separated by narrower bands of black and white scales. The tail and the outsides of the legs were spotted with white, the spots being fine and small on the legs, but so thickly distributed on the tail that in places they formed vertical bands. Its back was striped lengthwise in alternate stripes of black and canary yellow. As if that was not enough, the yellow stripes were broken in places by series of pinkish scales. Bright and glossy, the reptile looked as though it had just been varnished and was still sticky.

As the skink and I sat there and watched each other I worked out a plan for its capture. The butterfly net was some twenty feet away, but it might just as well have been in England for all the use it was, for I knew the skink would not lie there and allow me to trot over and fetch it. Behind the skink stretched a limitless jungle of long grass, and once it ran into that I knew it would disappear for good. Just then, to my dismay, I heard the Beagles returning, and I had to do something quickly, for their approach would frighten the reptile. Slowly I rose to my feet, and the skink raised its head in alarm. As the first of the Beagles trotted through the grass I flung myself desperately towards the skink. I had it at a slight disadvantage, for, having contemplated me in a motionless condition for a quarter of an hour, it had not expected me to launch myself through the air like a hawk. But my advantage was only temporary, for it recovered from its surprise quickly enough, and as I landed in the grass with a thump it scuttled to one side with great agility. I rolled over and made a wild grab at the rapidly retreating form, and as I did so a Beagle entered the clearing and saw what

I was doing. Instead of leaping to help me, as I had expected, he uttered a prolonged shriek, jumped forward, and proceeded to drag me away from my quarry. The skink scuttled off into the dense tangle of grass and was lost.

I shook off the Beagle's clutch on my arm and turned on him angrily. "Bushman, na what foolish ting you do, eh?"

"Masa," said the Beagle, clicking his fingers in agitation, "na bad bad beef dat ting. If 'e go bite Masa, Masa go die one time."

With an effort I controlled my irritation. I had long ago found that in spite of all arguments the Africans clung tenaciously to their belief that some harmless species of reptile were deadly poisonous. I resisted the effort to tell the Beagle he was an unmitigated idiot and tried another line of argument. "How you de call dis beef?" I asked.

"We call um que-fong-goo, sah."

"You say he get poison too much, eh?"

"Time no dere, Masa. Na bad beef."

"All right, stupid man, you done forget that European get special medicine for dis kind of beef, eh? You done forget if dis beef go bite me I no go die, eh?"

"Eh! Masa, I done forget dis ting."

"So you go run like women, you de hollar and you de hold me so I go lose dis fine beef because you forget, eh?"

"Sorry, sah," said the Beagle contritely.

I tapped his woolly skull with my finger. "Next time, my friend," I said sternly, "you go tink with your brain before you go do dis kind of ting, you hear?"

"I hear, sah."

When the other Beagles arrived on the scene the incident

was described to them, and there was much gasping and clicking of fingers. "Whah!" said one of them admiringly. "Masa no
get fear. 'E done try for catch que-fong-goo."

"An' Uano done catch Masa," said another, and they all
laughed uproariously.

"Ay, Uano, you get lucky today. Sometime Masa go kill
you for dis stupid ting," said another, and they went off into
fresh paroxysms of laughter at the thought of the Beagle's
having the temerity to stop me catching a specimen.

When they had recovered from the humour of the situation
I questioned them closely about the reptile. They assured me
that it was fairly common in the grasslands and I should have
plenty of opportunities of obtaining more specimens. They
were all agreed, however, on the deadly properties of the
skink. It was so poisonous, they said, that if you so much as
touched its body you immediately fell to the ground, writhing
in agony, and died within a few minutes. Then they asked
me about the medicine to counteract this deadly creature,
but I was suitably mysterious. I said that if they found me
a que-fong-goo I would catch it and prove to them that I
did not die writhing in agony. Cheered and intrigued by the
thought of this grisly experiment, for none of them really
believed in my medicine, they promised to do this. One Beagle
said he knew of a place not very far away where a great many
were to be found. So we packed up the equipment and set
off, the hunters chattering away to one another, presumably
laying bets as to whether or not I would survive an encounter
with a que-fong-goo.

The Beagle led us to a hillside about a mile away. The heavy
mountain rains had stripped most of the red earth from the

slope and left great sheets of grey rock exposed. Occasional clefts in the rock had allowed a pocket of earth to form, and in these grew such plants as could draw nourishment from so small an area of soil. The sheets of rock were hemmed in by tall golden grass and curious thistlelike plants with pale buttercup-yellow heads. The rock, lying exposed to the sun, was almost too hot to touch; the thin rubber soles on my shoes stuck to the surface as I walked across, and I felt as though I were walking across flypaper. I began to wonder if this baking rockface would not prove too much for even the most sun-loving of reptiles. Suddenly a flying streak of colour shot out of a clump of low growth, across the shimmering rock, and disappeared into the sanctuary of the long grass and thistles.

"Que-fong-goo!" said the Bafut Beagles, stopping short and clutching their spears more tightly.

Thinking that they would probably be more hindrance than help in any capture I might have to make, I told them to stay where they were and went ahead by myself. I had armed myself with a butterfly net, and as I cautiously approached the clumps of herbage that grew in the rock crevices I prodded them gently with the handle of the net to make sure there were no que-fong-goos lurking inside. It was quite astonishing what even a small clump of grass contained, and I disturbed innumerable large locusts, clouds of small moths and gnats, a mass of brilliant butterflies, some beetles, and a few dragonflies. I began to understand the attractions this scorched, barren place might have for lizards.

I was lucky: on inserting the net handle into a clump of grass and wiggling it gently I disturbed a que-fong-goo. It slithered out of hiding and skimmed across the rough surface of the rock as smoothly as a stone on ice. I gave chase but discovered almost immediately that a skink's idea of suitable country for sprinting was not mine. I caught my toe in a crack and fell flat on my face, and by the time I had picked myself up and recovered the net my quarry had disappeared. By now I was dripping with sweat, and the heat from the rock slabs was so great that any exertion made the blood pound in my head like a drum. The Beagles were standing at the edge of the long grass in a silent, fascinated group, watching my progress. I wiped my face, clutched the net in one sticky hand, and doggedly approached the next clump of grass. Here I was more careful: I edged the handle in among the grass stalks and moved it to and fro very gently and slowly, once or twice, and then withdrew it to see what would happen. I was rewarded by the sight of a que-fong-goo sticking its head cautiously out of the undergrowth to see what had caused the upheaval. Quickly I kicked the clump of grass behind it and swept the net down as it ran out. The next moment I lifted the net triumphantly with the que-fong-goo lashing furiously about in the folds. I pushed my hand inside the net and grabbed the reptile round the middle. It retaliated by fastening its jaws on my thumb. Though the jaws were powerful, the teeth were minute, so its bite was quite painless and harmless. To keep it occupied I let it chew away on my thumb while I lifted it from the net. I held the dazzlingly beautiful body aloft and waved it like a banner.

"Lookum," I shouted to the Beagles, who were watching me open-mouthed, "I done catch que-fong-goo!"

As the Beagles were carrying the soft cloth bags I used to transport reptiles I left the net lying on the rocks and walked towards them, clutching the skink in my hand. As one man, the Bafut Beagles dropped their spears and fled into the long grass like a herd of startled antelopes.

"What you de fear, eh?" I shouted. "I go hold um tight for my hand. I no go let um run."

"Masa, we de fear too much," they chorused, keeping a safe distance away.

"Bring me bag for dis beef," I ordered sternly, mopping my brow.

"Masa, we de fear. Na bad beef dat," came the cry again.

I had to produce a fairly stiff argument or else I should have to pursue my tribe of hunters all over the grasslands in my efforts to get a bag to put the skink in. I sat down at the edge of the long grass and glared at them.

"If someone no go bring me bag for put dis beef *one time*," I proclaimed loudly and angrily, "tomorrow I go get new hunter man. And if de Fon go ask me why I go do dis ting, I go tell him I want hunter man who no get fear, I no want women."

A silence descended upon the long grass while the Bafut Beagles decided whether it was better to face a que-fong-goo in the hand or a Fon at Bafut. After a short time the que-fong-goo won, and they approached me slowly and reluctantly. One of them, still keeping a safe distance, threw me a bag to put my capture in, but before I put the skink inside it I thought a little demonstration would be a good thing.

"Lookum," I said, holding the struggling lizard up for them to see. "Now you go watch fine and you see dis beef no get power for poison me."

Holding the skink in one hand, I slowly brought the forefinger of my other hand close to its nose; the reptile immediately gaped in a fearsome manner, and, amid cries of horror from the Beagles, I stuffed as much of my finger as I could into its mouth and let it chew.

The Bafut Beagles stood rooted to the spot, watching with expressions of incredulous stupefaction as the reptile gnawed away at my finger. Their eyes were wide, they held their breath and leaned slightly forward with open mouths as they watched to see if the creature's bite would have any effect. After a few seconds the que-fong-goo tired of biting ineffectually at my finger and let go. I dropped it neatly into the bag and tied up the neck.

"You see?" I inquired. "Dis beef done bite me, no be so?"

"Na so, sah," came in an awed whisper from the Beagles.

"All right. He done give me poison, eh? You tink sometime I go die, eh?"

"No, sah. If dat beef done bite Masa and Masa no die one time, den Masa no go die attall."

"Na dis special medicine I done get," I lied, shrugging with becoming modesty.

"Whah! Na so. Masa get fine medicine," said the Beagles.

I would like to point out that I had not gone through all this merely as a demonstration of the white man's superiority over the black; the reason for this little charade was that I wanted a great many que-fong-goos, and I knew that I should not get them unless I had the help and cooperation of the Beagles. To get this I had to overcome their fear of the reptile, and the only way I could do this was by showing them that my mythical medicine was more than a match for the deadly bite of the que-fong-goo. At some future date, I thought, I would provide them with a quantity of innocuous liquid disguised as the medicine in question, and, armed with this elixir, they would sally forth and return with sackfuls of glittering que-fong-goos.

On the way back to Bafut I strutted along, proudly carrying my precious skink and feeling very pleased with myself for having devised such a cunning scheme for obtaining more of the lovely reptiles. Behind me the Beagles trotted in silence, still gazing at me with awed expressions. Each time we passed someone on the path they would give a rapid résumé of my powers, and I would hear gasps of surprise and horror as the tale was told.

When we reached the villa and I had my skink nicely housed in a large box I gathered the Beagles together and made them a little speech. I pointed out that, as they had seen with their own eyes, my medicine was sufficient protection against the bites of que-fong-goos. They all nodded vigorously. Therefore, I went on, as I wanted a great many specimens of the reptile, I proposed to supply them with the magic potion the next day, and thus armed they would be able to go out and hunt que-fong-goos for me. I beamed at them complacently, waiting for the cries of delight I expected. None came. The Beagles stood there looking extremely glum and twiddling their toes in the dust.

"Well," I inquired after a long pause, "you no agree?"

"No, Masa," they mumbled.

"Why you no agree? You no savvay dat I go give you dis special medicine, eh? Why you de fear?"

They scratched their heads, shuffled their feet, glanced helplessly at one another. One of them at last plucked up the courage to speak. "Masa," he said, having cleared his throat several times, "dis medicine you done get na fine one. We savvay dis ting. We done see dis beef bite Masa time no dere, and Masa no die."

"Well?"

"Dis medicine, Masa, na juju for white man. No be juju for black man. For Masa na good ting dis medicine, but for we no be good ting."

For half an hour I argued, pleaded, and cajoled. They were polite but firm: the medicine was fine for whites but would not work for them. That was their belief and they were sticking to it. I tried every argument I could think of to make them change their minds, but it was no use. Thoroughly irritated by the failure of my little scheme, I dismissed the Beagles and stalked off to have my meal.

Later that evening the Fon turned up, accompanied by five council members and a bottle of gin. We sat on the moonlit veranda for half an hour or so, discussing various subjects in a desultory fashion, and then the Fon hitched his chair closer to mine and leaned forward, giving me the wide, engaging grin that lit up his whole face.

"Some man done tell me dat you done catch que-fong-goo," he said. "Dis man speak true?"

"Na so." I nodded. "Na fine beef dat."

"Dis man done say you catch dis beef with your hand," said the Fon. "I tink sometime dis man tell me lie, eh? Dis na bad beef, dis que-fong-goo, you no fit catch um with your hand, eh? 'E go kill you one time, no be so?"

"No," I said firmly, "dis man no tell lie. I done catch dis beef with my hand."

The council members let out their breath with a hiss, and the Fon sat back, wide-eyed, and regarded me. "An when you done catch um what 'e done do?" he asked.

"He done bite me."

"Whaaaah!" said the Fon and the council members in unison.

"He done bite me here," I said, holding out my hand.

The Fon shied away as though I had pointed a gun at him. He and the council members examined my finger from a safe distance, chattering eagerly to one another.

"Why you no die?" asked the Fon.

"Die?" I said, frowning. "Why I go die?"

"Na bad beef dis ting," said the Fon excitedly. " 'E de bite too much. If black man go hold him 'e go die one time. Why you never die, my friend?"

"Oh, I get special medicine for dis ting," I said airily.

A chorus of "ahhs!" came from my audience.

"Na European medicine dis?" asked the Fon.

"Yes. You like I go show you?"

"Yes, yes, na foine!" he said eagerly.

They sat in silent expectation while I went and fetched my small medicine chest. From it I extracted a packet of boracic powder and spread a little on the palm of my hand. They all craned eagerly forward to see. I filled a glass of water, mixed in the powder, then rubbed the solution on my hands.

"There," I said, spreading my hands out like a conjurer, "now que-fong-goo no fit kill me."

I walked over to the skink box, opened it, and turned round, holding the beast in my hands. There was a fluttering of robes as the council members fled to the other end of the veranda

in a disorderly stampede. The Fon remained rooted in his chair,
a look of disgust and fright on his face. I stopped in front of
him and held out the reptile, which was busily trying to ampu-
tate my finger.

"Look, you see?" I inquired. "Dis beef no fit kill me."

The Fon's breath escaped in a prolonged "aieeeeeee!" of
astonishment. Presently he tore his fascinated eyes away from
the lizard and looked up at me. "Dis medicine," he said hoarsely,
" 'e good for black man?"

"Na fine for black man."

"Black man no go die?"

"Attall, my friend."

The Fon sat back and gazed at me in wonder. "Whah" he
said at last, "na fine ting dis!"

"You like you go try dis medicine?" I asked casually.

"Er—er—yes, yes, na foine," said the Fon nervously.

Before he could change his mind I put the skink back in the
box and prepared more of the boracic mixture. I showed the
Fon how to rub it on his enormous hands, and he massaged
away for a long time. Then I brought the box, pulled out the
skink, and held it out.

It was a tense moment: the ring of council members watched
with bated breath and screwed-up countenances while the Fon
licked his lips, put out his hand, drew it back nervously, and
then reached out again. There was a moment's suspense as his
hand hovered over the reptile, and then he drew a deep breath
and grabbed it firmly round the waist.

"Ahhh!" hissed the councillors.

"Wheee! I done hold um," yelped the Fon, clutching the
unfortunate skink so tightly that I feared for its life.

"Hold um softly," I begged. "You go kill um if you hold um tight."

But the Fon, paralysed by a mixture of fright and pleasure at his own daring, could only sit there glaring at the skink in his hand and muttering, "I done hold um . . . I done hold um . . ." until I was forced to prise the unfortunate skink loose and return it to its box.

The Fon examined his hands and then looked up with an expression of childlike delight on his face. He waved his hands at me and started to laugh. He laughed and laughed and laughed, slapping his thighs, doubling up in his chair, coughing and spluttering, while the tears ran down his face. It was so infectious that I started to laugh too, and soon the councillors joined in. We sat there stamping our feet, laughing as though we would never stop, until some of the councillors rolled on the floor, fighting for breath, and the Fon lay back weakly in his chair.

"Why you de laugh?" I spluttered at last.

"Na funny ting," said the Fon, shaking with fresh laughter. "For long time, ever since I be picken, I done fear dis beef. Whah! I done fear um too much. Now you give me medicine and I no de fear any more." He leaned back in his chair and sobbed with mirth at the thought. "Que-fong-goo, your time done pass, I no go fear you again!"

Later, still aching from our laughter, we finished our drinks, and the Fon went back to his own villa, carefully clutching a small packet of boracic powder. I had warned him that, although the medicine could be used with success against que-fong-goos, agamas, and geckos, it could not, in any circumstances, be used to guard against the bite of snakes. As I had hoped, the story that the Fon had picked up a que-fong-goo, after having been immunized by my medicine, and survived the encounter was common gossip the next day.

In the afternoon the Bafut Beagles turned up and stood there grinning at me disarmingly.

"Whatee?" I asked coldly.

"Masa," said the Beagles, "give us dat medicine you done give for Fon, and we go hunt que-fong-goos for Masa."

That evening I had two boxes full of the beautiful grassland skinks, and the Bafut Beagles were drinking corn beer, surrounded by an admiring crowd of Bafutians, while they recounted the story of the day's hunt, with, I have no doubt, suitable embellishments. While I listened to them I sat on the veranda and wrote a note to the nearest United Africa Company stores, asking them to send me a supply of boracic. I felt that it might possibly come in useful.

8.   THE TYPHLOPS IN DISGUISE

Over a period of weeks the number of people who brought me
specimens dwindled to a steady daily trickle. This was due to
the fact that I had by this time obtained enough of the com-
moner species of animals and I was refusing to buy any more.
The veranda outside my bedroom was piled high with a strange
variety of cages, containing the most fantastically assorted
crowd of mammals, birds, and reptiles, and my mornings and
the better part of my evenings were devoted to their care. My
days were full but never dull. Apart from the cleaning and
feeding of the collection, there was endless enjoyment to be
got from watching the habits of my specimens, their reactions
to captivity and to myself. Then there was the life of Bafut.
Working on the veranda, I had an elevated vantage point commanding an excellent view of the road and the Fon's courtyard
and houses. Through the tattered fringe of bougainvillia I could
watch the movements of the Fon's numerous wives, offspring,

and councillors, and the constant comings and goings of the
Bafut population on the road. I observed many a scene enacted
below me, and by reaching out a hand for my field glasses I
could bring the actors so close that every slight change of expression on their faces could be noticed.

One evening I saw a slim, good-looking girl walk down the
road; she was meandering, dragging her feet, as though waiting
for someone to catch up with her. I was just about to call a
greeting to her as she passed beneath the house when a powerful young man came trotting up behind her, his face distorted
in a ferocious scowl, and called out sharply. The girl paused,
then turned round with an expression of sulky insolence on her
handsome face, which the young man obviously found very irritating. He halted in front of her and started to talk in a loud,
angry voice, gesturing fiercely with his arms, his eyes and teeth
flashing in his dark face. The girl stood without movement, a
faint, rather sneering smile on her lips.

Then a third actor joined the scene: an old woman came
scuttling down the road, screaming at the top of her voice and
waving a long bamboo. The man took no notice of the new-
comer but continued his rather one-sided argument with the
girl. The old woman danced round the two of them, brandish-
ing her bamboo, screeching shrilly, her flat, wrinkled dugs
flapping up and down on her chest as she moved. The more
she screeched the louder the man shouted, and the more he
shouted the more sullen became the girl's expression. Suddenly
the old woman whirled round on one leg like a dervish and
struck the man across the shoulders with her bamboo. The only
notice he took of this assault was to reach out a long, muscular
arm, twitch the stick from the old woman's hand and fling it

high into the air so that it fell over the red brick wall into the
courtyard. The old woman stood nonplussed for a moment,
then danced up behind the young man and kicked him hard in
the behind. He took no notice whatsoever, continuing to shout
at the girl, his gestures getting wilder and wilder. All at once
the girl snarled some reply at him and spat accurately on his
feet.

Up until then the young man had maintained a nonbelliger-
ent attitude, and he had, I felt, been getting the worst of things.
The women, I decided, were taking an unfair advantage of him.
Anyhow, having his feet spat upon was apparently the last
straw; he stood for a moment open-mouthed at such a treacherous attack, and then, with a roar of rage, he leaped forward,
grasped the girl round the throat with one hand, and with the
other boxed her ears soundly. Finally he gave her a push that
sent her to the ground. The old woman was quite overcome
by this action, fell flat on her back into the ditch, and indulged
in the finest fit of hysterics I have ever seen. Rolling from side
to side and patting her mouth, she gave vent to prolonged Red
Indian hoots of the most bloodcurdling quality. Occasionally
she would break off these noises to scream. The girl lay in the
red dust, sobbing bitterly. The man took no notice of the old
lady but squatted down beside the girl and appeared to be
pleading with her. After a while the girl looked up and gave a
watery smile, whereupon the young man sprang to his feet,
grabbed her by the wrist, and they set off down the road,
leaving the old woman rolling and hooting in the ditch.

I was, quite frankly, puzzled by the whole affair. What had
it all been about? Was the girl the man's wife, and had she been
unfaithful to him, and had he found out? But what, then, was

the reason for the old woman's presence? Perhaps the girl had stolen something from the man? Or, more likely, the girl and the old woman had been practising juju on him and he had found out? Juju, I thought, that must be the explanation. The girl, tiring of her young husband, had tried to poison him by mixing chopped-up leopard whiskers with his food, leopard whiskers she had obtained from the old woman, who was, of course, a well-known local witch. But the husband had become suspicious, and the girl had fled to the witch for protection. The husband had followed the girl, and the witch, who felt some sort of obligation towards her customers, had followed them both to try to sort things out. I had just worked this theory into a form that would have been acceptable even to the most lurid magazine when I looked over the edge of the veranda and saw Jacob below, peering through the hedge at the old woman rolling in the ditch.

"Jacob," I called, "na whatee all dat palaver?"

Jacob looked up and gave a throaty chuckle. "Dis ole woman, sah, she be mammy for dat picken woman. Dat picken woman be wife for dat man. Dat man 'e done go for bush all day, an' when 'e done come back 'e find 'e wife never make him food. 'E belly de cry out, an' de man angry too much, so he like beat 'e wife. De wife 'e run, de man 'e run for beat 'e wife, an' de ole woman 'e run for beat dis man."

I was bitterly disappointed. I felt that Africa, the dark, mysterious continent, had let me down. Instead of my juicy intrigue, my witches and magic potions full of leopard whiskers, I had been witnessing a common garden variety of domestic upheaval, with all the usual ingredients of an erring wife, a hungry husband, an uncooked dinner, and an interfering mother-in-law. I turned my attention back to the collection, feeling definitely cheated. It was the mother-in-law, I think, that rankled most.

Not long after this there was another upheaval on and around the veranda, in which I played a major role, but it was not until long afterwards that I was able to appreciate the humour of the situation. It was a beautiful evening, and in the west shoals of narrow, puffy clouds were assembling for what was obviously going to be a tremendous sunset. I had just finished a well-earned cup of tea and was sitting on the top step in the late sunlight, trying to teach an incredibly stupid baby squirrel how to suck milk from a blob of cotton wool on the end of a matchstick. Pausing for a moment in this nerve-racking work, I saw a fat, elderly woman waddling down the road. She was wearing the briefest of loincloths and was smoking a long slender black pipe. On top of her grey cropped hair perched a calabash. At the bottom step she knocked out her pipe and hung it carefully from the cord round her ample waist before starting to climb towards the veranda.

"Iseeya, mammy," I called.

She stopped and grinned up at me. "Iseeya, Masa," she replied, then continued to heave her body from step to step, panting and wheezing with the exertion. When she reached me she placed the calabash at my feet and leaned her bulk against the wall, gasping for breath.

"You done tire, mammy?" I asked.

"Whah! Masa, I get fat too much," she explained.

"Fat!" I said in shocked tones. "You no get fat, mammy. You no get fat pass me."

She chuckled richly, and her gigantic body quivered. "No, Masa, you go fun with me."

"No, mammy, I speak true. You be small woman."

She fell back against the wall, convulsed with laughter at the thought of being called a small woman, her vast stomach and breasts heaving. When she had recovered from the joke she gestured at the calabash. "I done bring beef for you, Masa."

"Na what kind of beef?"

"Na snake, Masa."

I unplugged the calabash and peered inside. Coiled up in the bottom was a thin brown-coloured snake about eight inches long. I recognized it as a typhlops, a species of blind snake which spends its life burrowing underground. It resembles the English slowworm in appearance and is quite harmless. I already had a box full of these reptiles, but I liked my fat girl friend so much I didn't want to disappoint her by refusing it. "How much you want for dis beef, mammy?" I asked.

"Eh, Masa go pay me how 'e tink."

"Snake no get wound?"

"No, Masa, attall."

I turned the calabash upside down, and the snake fell out on the smooth concrete. The woman moved to the other end of the veranda with a speed amazing for one so huge.

" 'E go bite you, Masa," she warned.

Jacob, who had come out to see what was going on, gave the woman a withering look. "You no savvay Masa no get fear for dis ting?" he asked. "Masa get special juju so dis kind of snake no go chop 'e."

"Ah, na so?" said the woman.

I leaned forward and picked up the typhlops in my hand, so that I could examine it closely to make sure it was unhurt. I gripped the body gently between my thumb and forefinger, and it twisted itself round my fingers. As I looked at it I noticed a curious thing: it possessed a pair of large, glittering eyes, a thing no typhlops ever possessed. Foolishly I still held the reptile loosely in my hand. "Jacob, look, dis snake 'e get eye," I said. As I spoke I suddenly realized that what I was holding in my hand was not a harmless typhlops but some unidentified snake of unknown potentialities. Before I could open my hand and drop it, the snake twisted round smoothly and buried a fang in the ball of my thumb.

Offhand I can never remember receiving quite such a shock. The bite itself was nothing, like the prick of a pin, followed by a slight burning sensation, rather similar to a wasp sting. I dropped the snake with alacrity and squeezed my thumb as hard as I could, so that the blood oozed out of the wound. As I squeezed I remembered three things: first, there was no snake-bite serum in the Cameroons; second, the nearest doctor was some thirty miles away; third, I had no means of getting to him. These thoughts did not make me feel any happier, and I sucked vigorously at the bite, holding the base of my thumb as tightly as I could. Looking about, I found that Jacob had vanished, and I was just about to utter a roar of rage when he came scurrying back, carrying a razorblade in one hand and a couple of ties in the other. Under my frenzied directions he tied the latter tightly round my wrist and forearm, and then, with a curious gesture, he handed me the razorblade.

I had never realized before quite how much determination it requires to slash yourself with a razorblade; nor had I realized

quite how sharp a razorblade could be. After an awful moment's hesitation I slashed at my hand, and found I had given
myself a nasty and unnecessary cut about half an inch away
from the bite, in a place where it could be of no possible use.
I tried again with much the same result, and I thought gloomily
that if I did not die of the bite I would probably bleed to death
as a result of my own first aid. I thought vindictively of all those
books I had read that gave tips on how to deal with snake bite.
All of them, without exception, told you how to make an
incision across the bite to the full depth of the fang punctures.
It's easy enough to write that sort of thing, but it's quite a different matter to put it successfully into practice when the thumb
you are slitting open is your own. There was only one thing
to be done, unless I wanted to go on hacking my hand in the
hopes of hitting the bite sooner or later. I placed the blade carefully on the ball of my thumb and, gritting my teeth, I pressed
and pulled as hard as I could. This was successful, and the blood
flowed freely in all directions. The next thing to do, I remembered, was to use permanganate of potash, and so I sprinkled
some crystals into the gaping wound and wrapped my hand
in a clean handkerchief. By now my hand, wrist, and the glands
in my armpit were considerably swollen, and there were shooting pains in my thumb, though whether this was due to the bite
or to my surgery I could not tell.

"Masa go for doctor?" asked Jacob, staring at my hand.

"How I go for doctor?" I asked irritably. "We no get car
for dis place. You tink sometimes I go walk?"

"Masa go ask de Fon for 'e kitcar," suggested Jacob.

"Kitcar?" I repeated, hope dawning. "De Fon get kitcar?"

"Yes, sah."

"Go ask him den—one time."

Jacob galloped down the steps and across the courtyard, while I paced up and down on the veranda. Suddenly I remembered that in my bedroom reposed an untouched bottle of French brandy, and I sped inside in search of it. I had just managed to pull out the cork when I recalled that all the books on snake bite were adamant when it came to the point of spirits. On no account, they all stated, must spirits be taken by anyone suffering from snake bite; it accelerated the heart action and did all sorts of other strange things to you. For a moment I paused, the bottle clutched in one hand; then I decided that if I was going to die I might as well die happy, and I raised the bottle and drank. Warmed and encouraged, I trotted out to the veranda again, carrying the bottle with me.

A large crowd of people, headed by Jacob and the Fon, were hurrying across the courtyard. They went over to a large hut, and the Fon threw open the door and the crowd poured inside, to reappear almost immediately, pushing in front of them an ancient and battered kitcar. They trundled this out through the archway and into the road, and there the Fon left them and hurried up the steps, followed by Jacob.

"My friend," said the Fon, "na bad palaver dis!"

"Na so," I admitted.

"Your boy done tell me you no get European medicine for dis kind of bite, na so?"

"Yes, na so. Sometime doctor done get medicine. I no savvay."

"By God power 'e go give you medicine," said the Fon piously.

"You go drink with me?" I asked, waving the bottle of brandy.

"Yes, yes," said the Fon, brightening, "we go drink. Drink na good medicine for dis kind of ting."

Jacob brought glasses, and I poured out a liberal measure for us both. Then we went to the top of the steps to see what progress was being made.

The ambulance had reposed inside the hut for such a great length of time that its internal organs appeared to have jammed up. Under the driver's gentle ministrations the engine coughed vigorously several times and then ceased. The large crowd round the vehicle clustered closer, all shouting instructions to him, while he leaned out the window and abused them roundly. Then the driver climbed out and tried to crank her up. This was even less successful, and when he had exhausted himself he handed the crank to a councillor and sat down on the running board for a rest. The councillor hitched up his robes and struggled manfully with the crank but was unable to rouse the engine to life. The crowd, which now numbered about fifty people, all clamoured for a turn, and the councillor handed the job over to them and joined the driver on the running board. A disgraceful fight broke out among the crowd as to who should have first turn, and everyone was shouting and pushing and snatching the crank.

The uproar attracted the attention of the Fon. He drained his glass and stalked over to the veranda rail, scowling angrily. "Whah!" he roared. "Start dat motor!"

The crowd fell silent, and all turned to look up at the veranda, while the driver and the council member jumped off the running board and rushed round to the front of the car with an amazing display of enthusiasm. The effect was somewhat spoiled by the fact that the crank was missing. Uproar started again, with everyone accusing everyone else of having lost it. It was found eventually, and the two of them made several more ineffectual attempts to get the engine started.

By now I was beginning to feel rather ill and not at all brave. My hand and forearm had swollen considerably and were inflamed and painful. I was also getting shooting pains across my shoulders, and my hand felt as though it were grasping a red-hot coal. It would take me about an hour to reach the doctor, I thought, and if the kitcar did not start soon there would be little point in going at all.

The driver, having nearly ruptured himself in his efforts to crank, was suddenly struck by a brilliant idea. They would push the car. His idea was greeted with exclamations of delight and acclamation. The driver got in, and the crowd swarmed round behind the kitcar and started to push. Grunting rhythmically, they pushed the kitcar slowly down the road, round the corner, and out of sight.

"Soon 'e go start." The Fon smiled encouragingly, pouring me some more brandy. "Den you go reach doctor one time."

"You tink 'e go start?" I asked sceptically.

"Yes, yes, my friend," said the Fon, looking hurt. "Na my kitcar dis. Na foine one. 'E go start small time, no go fear."

Soon we heard the grunting again, and on looking over the veranda rail we saw the kitcar appear round the corner, propelled by what appeared to be the entire population of Bafut. It crept towards us like a snail, and then, just as it reached the bottom step, the engine gave a couple of preliminary hiccups and roared into life. The crowd screamed with delight and capered about in the road.

"'E done start," explained the Fon proudly, in case I had missed the point of the celebrations.

The driver manoeuvred the car through the archway into the courtyard, turned her round, and swept out on the road again, impatiently tootling his horn and narrowly missing his erstwhile helpers.

The Fon and I drained our glasses and marched down the seventy-five steps. At the bottom the Fon clasped me to his bosom and gazed earnestly into my face. It was obvious that he wanted to say something that would encourage and sustain me on my journey. He thought deeply for a moment. "My friend," he said at last, "if you go die I get sorry too much."

Not daring to trust my voice, I clasped his hand in what I hoped was a suitably affecting manner, climbed into the kit-car, and we were off, bouncing and jerking down the road, leaving the Fon and his subjects enveloped in a cloud of red dust.

Three-quarters of an hour later we drew up before the doctor's house with an impressive squealing of brakes. The doctor was standing outside gloomily surveying a flower bed. He looked at me in surprise, and then, coming forward to greet me, he peered closely into my face.

"What have you been bitten by?" he inquired.

"How did you know I'd been bitten?" I asked, rather startled by his rapid diagnosis.

"Your pupils are tremendously distended," explained the doctor with professional relish. "What was it?"

"A snake. I don't know what kind, but it hurts like hell. I don't suppose there was really much use in my coming in to you. There's no serum to be had, is there?"

"Well," he said in a pleased tone of voice, "isn't that a strange thing! Last time I was on leave I got some serum. Thought it might come in useful. It's been sitting in the fridge for the last six months."

"Thank heaven for that."

"Come into the house. I shall be most interested to see if it works."

"So shall I," I admitted.

We went into the house, and the doctor and his wife sat me down in a chair while they busied themselves with methylated spirits, hypodermic needles, and the other accoutrements necessary for the operation. Then the doctor gave me three injections in the thumb, as near to the bite as possible, and a couple in my arm. These hurt considerably more than the original bite had done.

"Made you feel a bit rocky?" inquired the doctor cheerfully, feeling my pulse.

"They've made me feel bloody," I said bitterly.

"What you need is a good stiff whisky."

"I thought one wasn't allowed spirits?"

"Oh yes. It won't hurt you," he said and poured me out a glassful.

I can never remember a drink tasting so good.

"And now," the doctor went on, "you're to spend the night in the spare room. I want you in bed in five minutes. You can have a bath if you feel like it."

"Can't I go back to Bafut?" I asked. "I've got all my animals there, and there's no one really competent to look after them."

"You're in no state to go back to Bafut or to look after animals," he said firmly. "Now no arguments, into bed. You can go back in the morning if I think you're well enough."

To my surprise, I slept soundly, and when I awoke the next day I felt extremely well, though my arm was still swollen and mildly painful. I had breakfast in bed, and then the doctor came to have a look at me.

"How d'you feel?" he asked.

"Fine. I'm feeling so well that I'm beginning to think the snake must have been harmless."

"No, it was poisonous, all right. You said it only got you with one fang, and you probably dropped it so quickly that it didn't have time to inject the full shot of venom. If it had, it might have been another story."

"Can I go back to Bafut?"

"Well, yes, if you feel up to it, but I shouldn't think that arm will be up to much for a day or two. Anyway, if it worries you, come in and see me."

Spurred on by the thought of my precious collection waiting at Bafut, uncleaned and unfed, I goaded the unfortunate driver so that he got us back in record time. As we drew up below the villa I saw a figure seated on the bottom step. It was my fat girl friend of the day before.

"Iseeya, mammy," I said, stepping down to the road.

"Iseeya, Masa," she replied, hoisting herself to her feet and waddling towards me.

"Na what you de want?" I asked, for I was impatient to get up to my animals.

"Masa done forget?" she inquired, surprised.

"Forget what, mammy?"

"Eh, Masa!" she said accusingly. "Masa never pay me for dat fine snake I done bring."

9.   THE FON AND THE GOLDEN CAT

My stay in Bafut eventually drew to a close. I had collected
a vast quantity of animal life, and it was time to take it all back
to the base camp, where it could be recaged and got ready
for the voyage. Reluctantly I informed the hunters that I
would be leaving in a week, so that they would not bring in
any specimens after I had left. I ordered the lorry and sent a
note to Smith, telling him to expect me. The Fon, when he
heard the news, came flying over, clasping a bottle of gin, and
did his best to persuade me to stay on. But, as I explained to him,
I could not stay any longer, much as I would like to; our return
passages were booked, and that meant the whole collection
had to be ready to move down country on the prescribed date.
If there was any hitch we would miss the ship, and we might
not be able to get another one for a couple of months, a delay
which the trip's budget was not designed to cope with.

"Ah! My friend, I sorry too much you go," said the Fon, pouring gin into my glass with the gay abandon of a fountain.

"I sorry too much as well," I said with truth, "but I no get chance for stay Bafut any more."

"You go remember Bafut," said the Fon, pointing a long finger at me. "You go remember Bafut fine. Na for Bafut you done get plenty fine beef, no be so?"

"Na so," I said, pointing at my vast piles of cages, "I done get beef too much for Bafut."

The Fon nodded benignly, leaned forward, and clasped my hand. "When you go for your country, sometime you go tell your people de Fon of Bafut na your friend, an 'e done get you all dis fine beef, eh?"

"I go tell um all," I promised, "and I go tell um dat de Fon be fine hunter man, better pass all hunter for Cameroons."

"Foine, foine!" said the Fon delightedly.

"Na one beef I never get for here," I said. "I sorry too much."

"Na whatee, my friend?"

"Na dat big bushcat dat get skin like gold and mark mark for 'e belly. I done show you photograph, you remember?"

"Ah! Dat beef! You speak true. Dat beef you never get yet."

He relapsed into a gloomy silence and scowled at the gin bottle. I wondered if reminding him of this gap in my collection had not been a little tactless. The animal to which I was referring was the golden cat, one of the smaller, but one of the most beautiful, members of the cat family to be found in that part of Africa. I knew that it was reasonably common around Bafut, but the hunters treated it with more respect than they did the serval and the leopard, both of which were considerably bigger. Whenever I had shown the hunters pictures of the beast they had chuckled and shaken their heads and assured me that it was extremely difficult to catch, that it was "fierce too much" and that it "get plenty clever." In vain I had offered large rewards, not only for the animal's capture, but for news of its whereabouts. With slightly less than a week to go before I left, I had resigned myself to not having a golden cat in the collection.

The Fon sat back in his chair with a twinkle in his eye and grinned at me infectiously. "I go get you dat beef," he said.

"But, my friend, in five days I go leave Bafut. How you go catch dis beef in five days?"

"I go catch um," said the Fon firmly. "Wait small time, you go see. I go get you dat beef."

He refused to tell me by what methods he was going to bring about this miracle, but he was so sure of himself that I began to wonder if he really would be able to get me one. When, however, the day before my departure dawned and there was still no sign of any golden cat, I gave up all hope. In his enthusiasm the Fon had made a promise he could not fulfil.

It was a sombre, overcast day, for up there in the mountains the rainy season started earlier than in the lowlands. The low, fast-moving clouds, grey as slate, the thin drizzle of rain, the occasional shudder of thunder in the distant mountain ranges— none of these things helped make me feel any the less depressed at the thought of leaving Bafut. I had grown very fond of this silent grassland world, and of the people who lived there. The Fon I had come to admire and like, and I felt genuinely sorry at the thought of saying good-bye to him, for he had been an amusing and charming companion.

About four o'clock the fine drizzle turned into a steady downpour that blurred the landscape, drummed and rattled on the roof of the villa and the fronds of the palm trees nearby, turned the red earth of the courtyard into a shimmering sea of blood-red clay freckled with pockmarks of the falling rain. I had finished my cleaning and feeding of the collection and was wandering moodily up and down the veranda, watching the rain beat and bruise the scarlet bougainvillia flowers against the brickwork. My luggage was packed, the cages were stacked and ready for loading into the lorry. I could think of nothing to do, and I did not fancy venturing out into the icy downpour.

Glancing down at the road, I saw a man appear at a trot, slipping and sliding in the mud, carrying a large sack on his back. Hoping that he was bringing me some rare specimen to lighten my gloom, I watched his approach eagerly, but to my annoyance he turned off under the archway, splashed across the courtyard, and disappeared through the arched door leading to the Fon's quarters. Shortly after he had vanished a great uproar broke out near the Fon's small villa, but it died down after some minutes, and all I could hear was the rain.

I drank my tea in solitary state, then finished feeding the nocturnal creatures. They seemed a trifle surprised, for I never fed them as early as that as a rule, but the Fon was coming over to spend the evening and I wanted to have everything done before he arrived. By the time I had finished my work the rain had died away to a fine mistlike drizzle, and through breaks in the low-flying grey clouds the sky shone a pale and limpid blue.

Within an hour the clouds had dispersed altogether, and the sky was smooth and clear and full of evening sunlight. A small drum started to beat over near the Fon's house, and the sound gradually grew louder. The door into the courtyard opened, and a small procession marched through. First came the Fon, dressed in magnificent scarlet and white robes, striding delicately through the shining puddles. Following him marched the strange man I had seen in the rain, still with the sack on his back. Behind him were four council members, and at the end of the procession trotted a small boy in white robes and minute skullcap, beating importantly on a little drum. The Fon was coming to pay me his last visit in style. I went down the steps to meet him.

He halted in front of me and put his hands on my shoulders, staring into my face with a most impressive sternness. "My friend," he said slowly and solemnly, "I done get something for you."

"Na whatee?" I asked.

The Fon flung back his trailing sleeves with a regal gesture and pointed at the man with the sack.

"Bushcat!" he said.

"Bushcat? Dat kind I de want too much?" I hardly dared to believe it.

The Fon nodded with the quiet satisfaction of one who has done a job well.

"Let me look um," I said excitedly. "Quick, open dat bag!"

The man placed the sack on the ground in front of me, and I, unmindful of the clean trousers I had put on in the Fon's honour, went down on my knees in the mud and struggled with the tough cord that bound the neck of the sack. The Fon stood beaming down at me like a benevolent Santa Claus. The cord was wet and tight, and as I tugged and pulled, a weird, ferocious cry arose from the interior of the sack: it started as a rumbling moan, and as it became louder it developed into a jarring scream with such a malevolent undertone that it sent a chill up my spine. The hunter, the councillors, and the boy with the drum retreated several paces.

"Careful, Masa," the hunter warned, "na bad beef dat. 'E get power too much."

"You done get rope for 'e foot?" I asked, and he nodded. I unwound the last bit of cord, slowly opened the sack, and peered inside.

Glaring up at me was a face of such beauty that I gasped. The fur was short, smooth, the rich golden brown of wild honey. The pointed ears were flattened close to the skull, and the upper lip was drawn back in a series of fine ripples from milk-white teeth and pink gums. But it was the eyes I noticed more than anything else: large, and set at a slight slant in the golden face,

they stared up at me with a look of such cold fury that I was
thankful the animal's feet were tied. They were green, the green
of leaves under ice, and they glittered like mica in the evening
sun. For a second we stared at each other, and then the golden
cat drew back her lips even farther away from her gums, opened
her mouth, and gave another loud, frightening cry. Hastily I
tied up the sack again, for I did not know if her bonds were
really strong or not, and, judging by her eyes, she would not
deal with me very kindly if she got free.

"You like?" asked the Fon.

"Whah! I like dis beef too much," I replied.

We carried the precious sack up to the veranda, and I turned
a specimen out of the largest, strongest cage I had. Then we
emptied the golden cat gently out of the sack and rolled her
inside, shutting and bolting the door. She lay on her side, hissing
and snarling but unable to move, for her front and back legs
were neatly tied together with strong raffialike cord. By fixing
a knife to the end of a stick I managed to saw through the cords,
and as they fell away she got to her feet in one smooth movement, leaped at the bars, stuck a fat golden paw through, and
took a swipe at my face. I drew back just in time.

"Aha," said the Fon, chuckling, "dis beef get angry too
much."

" 'E fit chop man time no dere," said the hunter.

" 'E get power," agreed the Fon, nodding. " 'E get plenty
power for 'e foot. You go watch um, my friend, less 'e go
wound you."

I sent down to the kitchen for a small chicken, and this,
freshly killed and warm, I dangled near the bars of the cage.
A golden paw again shot out between the bars, white claws

buried themselves in the fowl, and it was jerked up against the bars. Leaning forward, the cat got a grip on the neck of the bird, and with one quick heave the entire fowl vanished into the interior of the cage. Clouds of feathers poured out from between the bars as the golden cat began to feed. Reverently I covered the front of the cage with a sack, and we left her in peace to enjoy her meal.

"How you done catch dis beef?" I asked the hunter. He gave a grin and wiggled his toes with embarrassment.

"You no de hear?" asked the Fon. "You no get mouth? Speak now!"

"Masa," began the man, scratching his stomach, "de Fon done tell me Masa want dis kind of beef too much, an' so three days I done go for bush, I look um. I done walker, walker, I done tire too much, but I never see dis beef. Yesterday, for evening time, dis bushcat 'e done come softly for my farm, an' 'e done chop three chicken. Dis morning I see 'e foot for de mud, an' I done follow for bush. Far too much I done follow um, Masa, an' den, for some big hill, I done see um."

The Fon shifted in his chair and fixed the man with a glittering eye. "You speak true?" he asked sternly.

"Yes, Masa," protested the hunter, "I speak true."

"Good," said the Fon.

"I done see dis bushcat," the man went on. " 'E done walker for dis big hill. Den 'e done go for some place dere be rock too much. 'E done go for hole in de ground. I look dis hole, but man no fit pass, 'e tight too much. I done go back for my house an' I done bring fine dog and catch net, den I go back for dis place. I done put catch net for de hole, an' den I done make small fire an' put smoke for de hole."

He paused and hopped on one leg, clicking his fingers. "Whah! Dat beef fierce too much! When 'e done smell de smoke 'e de holler an' 'e de holler, time no dere. My dog dey de fear an' dey all done run. I de fear bushcat go catch me an' I done run also. Small time I hear de beef 'e holler an' holler, an' so I done go softly softly for look um. Whah! Masa, da beef 'e run run for inside catch net, an' de catch net done hold um fine. When I see um for catch net I no get fear again, an' so I done go an' I tie 'e foot with rope, an' I done bring um one time for Masa."

The man ended his story and stood watching us anxiously, twisting his short spear in both hands.

"My friend," I told him, "I tink you be fine hunter man, an' I go pay you good money for dis beef."

"Na so, na so," agreed the Fon, waving a lordly hand. "Dis man done make fine hunting for you."

I paid him a handsome sum of money and made him a present of several packets of cigarettes, and he went off grinning and saying "Tank you, Masa, tank you," all the way down the steps and along the road until he was out of earshot.

Then I turned to the Fon, who was sitting back watching me with a smug expression on his face. "My friend, I tank you too much for dis ting you done do," I said.

The Fon waved his hands. "No, no, my friend, na small ting dis. It no be good ting if you go leave Bafut and you never get all de beef you want. I sorry too much you do go leave. But when you look dis fine beef you go tink of Bafut, no be so?"

"Na true," I said. "And now, my friend, you go drink with me?"

"Foine, foine," said the Fon.

As if to compensate for the dreariness of the early part of the day the sunset was one of the finest I have ever seen. The sun sank down behind a grid of pale elongated clouds, and as it sank, the clouds turned from white to pearly pink, and then flushed to crimson edged with gold. The sky itself was washed with palest blues and greens, smudged here and there with a touch of gold. Pale trembling stars gained strength as the world darkened. Presently the moon came up, blood red at first, changing to yellow and then silver as it rose, turning the world a frosty silver, with shadows as black as charcoal.

The Fon and I sat drinking in the misty moonlight until it was late. Then he turned to me, pointing towards his villa. "I tink sometime you like to dance," he said, "so I done tell um to make musica. You like we go dance before you leave, eh?"

"Yes, I like to dance," I said.

The Fon lurched to his feet and, leaning perilously over the

veranda rail, shouted an order to someone waiting below. In a
short time a cluster of lights moved across the great courtyard,
and the Fon's all-female band assembled in the road below and
started to play. Soon they were joined by numerous others,
including most of the council members.

The Fon listened to the music for a bit, waving his hands and
smiling, and then got up and held out his hand to me. "Come!"
he said, "we go dance, eh?"

"Foine, foine!" I mimicked him, and he crowed with glee.

We made our way across the moon-misty veranda to the head
of the steps, the Fon draped a long arm over my shoulders,
partly out of affection and partly for support, and we started
to descend. Halfway down my companion stopped to execute
a short dance to the music. His foot got tangled up in his impressive robes, and, but for his firm grip round my neck, he would
have rolled down the steps into the road. As it was, we struggled
there for a moment, swaying violently, trying to regain our balance. The crowd of wives, offspring, and councillors gasped
in horror and consternation at the sight of their lord in such
peril, and the band stopped playing.

"Musica, musica!" roared the Fon as we reeled together on
the steps. "Why you done stop, eh?"

The band started up again. We regained our equilibrium and
walked down the rest of the way without mishap. The Fon
was in fine fettle, and he insisted on holding my hand and dancing across the courtyard, splashing through the puddles, while
the band trotted behind, playing a trifle short-windedly. When
we reached the dancing hut he sat down on his throne for a rest,
while his court took the floor. When there was a slight lull in
the dancing I asked the Fon if he would call the band over, so

that I could examine the instruments more closely. They trooped over and stood in front of the dais on which we sat.

I tried each instrument in turn and was shown the correct way of playing it. To everyone's surprise, including my own, I succeeded in playing the first few bars of "The Campbells Are Coming" on a bamboo flute. The Fon was so delighted he made me repeat it several times, while he accompanied me on a big drum, and one of the council members on the strange foghornlike instrument. The effect was not altogether musical, but we rendered it with great verve and feeling. Then we had to repeat it all over again, so that the Fon could hear how it sounded with a full band accompaniment. Actually, it sounded rather good, as most of my flat notes were drowned by the drums.

When we had exhausted the musical possibilities of the tune the Fon sent for another bottle, and we settled down to watch the dancers. The inactivity soon told on my companion, and after an hour or so he started to shift on his throne and to scowl at the band.

"Dis dance no be good," he confided at last.

"Na fine," I said. "Why you no like?"

" 'E slow too much," he pointed out and smiled at me disarmingly. "You like we go dance your special dance?"

"Special dance?" I queried, slightly fuddled. "What dance?"

"One, two, three, keek—one, two, three, keek," yodelled the Fon.

"Ah, dat dance you de talk. Yes, we go dance um if you like."

"I like too much," said the Fon firmly.

He led the way to the dance floor and clutched my waist in a firm grip, while everyone else, chattering and grinning with

delight, joined on behind. To add a little variety to the affair I
borrowed a flute and piped noisily and inaccurately on it as I
led them on a wild dance round the dance hall and out among
the huts of the Fon's wives. The night was warm, and half an
hour of this exercise made me stream with sweat and gasp for
breath.

We stopped for a rest and some liquid refreshment. It was
obvious, however, that my conga had got into the Fon's blood.
He sat on his throne, his eyes gleaming, feet tapping, humming
reminiscently to himself—and waiting with ill-concealed im-
patience until I had recovered my breath before suggesting that
we repeat the whole performance. I decided that I would have
to head him off in some way, for I found the conga too enervat-
ing for such a close night, and I had barked my shin quite pain-
fully on a doorpost during our last round. I cast around in my
mind for another dance I could teach him which would be less
strenuous to perform, and yet whose tune could easily be mas-
tered by the band. I made my choice, called once more for a
flute, and practiced on it for a few minutes.

Then I turned to the Fon, who had been watching me with
great interest. "If you go tell de band 'e go learn dis special
music I go teach you other European dance," I said.

"Ah! Foine, foine!" He roared the band to silence, then marshalled them round the dais.

I played the tune to them, and in a surprisingly short space
of time they had picked it up and were even adding little vari-
ations of their own.

The Fon stamped his feet delightedly. "Na fine music dis,"
he said, "now you go show me dis dance, eh?"

I looked round and singled out a young damsel who, I had

noticed, seemed exceptionally bright, and, clasping her as closely as propriety would permit (for her clothing was non-existent), I set off across the dance floor in a dashing polka. My partner after only a momentary hesitation picked up the step perfectly, and we bobbed and hopped round in great style. To show his appreciation the Fon started to clap, and immediately the rest of the court followed suit; it started off as normal, ragged applause, but, being Africans, they kept clapping and worked it into the rhythm of the dance. The girl and I circled round the large floor five times, and then we were forced to stop for a rest.

When I reached the dais the Fon held out a brimming glass of whisky and clapped me on the back as I sat down. "Na foine dance!" he said.

I nodded and gulped down my drink. As soon as I had put my glass down the Fon seized me by the hand and pulled me onto the floor again. "Come," he said persuasively, "you go show me dis dance."

Clasped in each other's arms, we polkaed round the room, but it was not a great success, owing chiefly to the fact that my partner's robes became entangled with my feet and jerked us both to a standstill. We would then have to stand patiently while a crowd of council members unwound us, after which we would go again: one, two, three, hop, only to end up in the opposite corner entwined together like a couple of maypoles.

Eventually I glanced at my watch and discovered to my dismay that it was three o'clock. Reluctantly I had to take my leave of the Fon and retire to bed. He and the court followed me out into the great courtyard. As I climbed up the steps to the villa I looked back at them. In among the twinkling hurricane lanterns they were all dancing the polka. In the centre the Fon was jigging and hopping by himself, waving one long arm and shouting, "Good night, my friend! Good night!" I waved back, and then went and crawled thankfully into my bed.

By eight-thirty the next morning the lorry had arrived and the collection had been stacked on it. An incredible number of Bafutians had come to say good-bye and to see me off; they had been arriving since early that morning, and now lined the road-side, chattering together, waiting for me to depart. The last load was hoisted onto the lorry, and the sound of drums, flutes, and rattles heralded the arrival of the Fon to take his leave of me. He was dressed as I had seen him on the day of my arrival, in a plain white robe and a wine-red skullcap. He was accom-panied by his retinue of councillors. He strode up and embraced me, and then, holding me by the hand, addressed the assembled Bafutians in a few rapid sentences. When he stopped the crowd broke into loud "arrrs" and started to clap rhythmically.

The Fon turned to me and raised his voice. "My people 'e sorry too much you go leave Bafut. All dis people dey go re-member you, and you no go forget Bafut, eh?"

"I never go forget Bafut," I said truthfully, making myself heard with difficulty above the loud, steady clapping of those hundreds of black hands.

"Good," he said with satisfaction. He clasped my hand firmly in his and wrung it. "My friend, always I go get you for my eye. I no go forget dis happy time we done get. By God power you go reach your own country safe. Walker good, my friend, walker good."

As the lorry started off down the road the clapping got faster and faster, until it sounded like rain on a tin roof. We jolted our way slowly along until we reached the corner. Looking back, I saw the road lined with naked black humanity, their hands fluttering as they clapped, and at the end of this avenue of moving hands and flashing teeth stood a tall figure in dazzling white. The Fon raised a long arm, and a huge hand waved a last farewell as the lorry rounded the corner and started up the red earth road that wound over the golden hills.

10.   ZOO UNDER CANVAS

One of the most frustrating things about collecting, from the collector's point of view, is the fact that he rarely gets to know any of his animals until towards the end of a trip. During the first four months or so they are just specimens to him, for he has not the time to observe them closely. He sees that they are adequately housed, feeds and cleans them, but beyond that he cannot go, for all his spare time is spent in trying to add to his menagerie. Towards the end of a trip, however, his collection has grown to such proportions that he cannot wander far afield, for he has too much to do. That is the time he has to rely entirely on the native hunters to bring in new specimens, and he, being confined to camp all day, has the opportunity of getting to know the creatures he has already assembled. Our collection had reached this point when I returned from Bafut. Not only had we the grassland animals, but during my stay in the mountains Smith had been steadily increasing the collection with the local forest fauna. Under the great canvas roof of our marquee we had a varied enough collection of creatures to start a small zoo.

On my return to our hot, humid base camp on the banks of the Cross River I began to appreciate some of my grassland captures for the first time. For example, take the case of the hyrax. Until I got them down to base camp I had considered them rather dull creatures, whose only claim to fame was their relatives. At first glance one would be pardoned for mistaking a hyrax for an ordinary member of the rodent family, and as you watched them nibbling away at leaves or gnawing at some juicy bark you would probably hazard a guess that they were related to the rabbits. In this you would be quite wrong, for a hyrax is an ungulate, an order that includes cattle, deer, swine, and horses; and the nearest relative to the hyrax is not the rabbit but the elephant, of all unlikely things. In the bone formation of the feet and in other anatomical details the hyrax is classified as coming closer to the elephant and the rhino than anything else. This is the sort of information that makes people wonder whether zoologists are quite sane, for a hyrax resembles an elephant about as closely as an elephant does a hummingbird. However, the relationship is clearer if one goes into the more complicated details of anatomy and dentition. This, frankly, was all the information I had about the hyrax.

When I reached base camp the female hyrax, which had savaged the Beagle's foot, and her two fat babies were transferred from the small cage they had been confined in to a much bigger affair that gave them plenty of space to move about in and had a private bedroom to which to retire if they felt in any way antisocial. In this cage I noticed several things I had not observed before. To begin with, they had what are called "lavatory habits"; that is to say, they always deposited their dirt in one spot in the cage. Until then I had not realized what a godsend

an animal with these habits could be to a hard-working collector. As soon as I had grasped the meaning of the neat little pile
of dung in the corner of the cage each morning, I provided
them with a round, shallow tin as a latrine. To my annoyance,
the next morning I found they had spurned my offer; they had
simply pushed the tin out of the way and deposited their dirt
in the usual place. That night I put the tin in again, but this time
I placed a few of their droppings in the bottom. The following
day the tin was piled high and the floor of the cage was spotless.
After that, the cleaning of the cage took approximately five
minutes: you emptied the tin, washed it, and put it back in
the corner. It became a real pleasure to clean out the hyrax.

As a contrast in habits there were the pouched rats. These
rodents, each as large as a small kitten, lived in the cage next
door to the hyrax family. They belonged to that irritating group
of beasts that won't—or can't—evacuate their bowels unless it
is done into water, preferably running water. In the wild state
they would probably use a stream, and the current would carry
the dirt away to fertilize some plant farther downstream. In a
cage, however, I could not provide the pouched rats with a
stream, and so they used the next best thing, which was their
water pot. There is nothing quite so frustrating as putting a
nice clean water pot, brimming with clear liquid, into a cage,
and, on looking at it five minutes later, finding that it resembles
a pot full of liquid manure. It was very worrisome, for in the
heat the animals needed a constant supply of fresh drinking
water. After many futile attempts to get them to relinquish this
habit, I supplied them with a large pot of water as a lavatory and
plenty of juicy fruit to eat, in the hope that this would quench
their thirst.

But to return to the hyrax. In Bafut I had decided that they were dull, unfriendly animals that spent their whole lives sitting on their haunches, chewing leaves, with a glazed look in their eyes. At base camp I discovered that I was quite mistaken, for the hyrax can be as lively as lambs when they put their minds to it. In the evening, when their cage was flooded with sunlight, the old female would lie there looking as imposing as a Trafalgar Square lion, munching methodically at a bunch of tender spinach or a cluster of cassava leaves, while her babies played with each other. These were wild and exhilarating romps round and round the cage; they sometimes astonished me by running straight up the smooth wooden back of the cage until they reached the roof, before dropping onto the floor. When they tired of these Wall of Death stunts they would use their mother's portly, recumbent body as a castle. One would climb up onto her back, while the other one attacked and tried to knock him off. Occasionally they would both be on their mother's back together, locked in mortal combat, while their parent lay there unmoved, chewing steadily, a trancelike look on her face. These games were delightful to watch, but there was one irksome thing, and that was the babies would sometimes carry on far into the night, especially if there was a moon. It is extremely difficult to get to sleep when a pair of baby hyrax are dashing about their cage, producing a noise like a couple of stallions fighting in a loose box. Sitting up in bed and shouting *"Shut up"* in fearsome tones had the effect of stopping them for about half an hour; if you had not drifted into sleep by then, you would be brought back to life by the thumping of wood, twanging of wire, and the melodious crash of food pots being kicked over. The hyraxes were certainly anything but dull.

Another creature that started to blossom into his true colours when we arrived at base camp was the black-eared squirrel, the beast that had created such havoc on the steps of the villa in Bafut. This episode of the steps was, if I had only known it at the time, but a slight indication of what he could do, for his one delight in life seemed to be escaping and being chased by a crowd of people. He was, as I have already mentioned, quite a baby, and within a very short time after his arrival he had become extraordinarily tame and would allow me to pick him up and place him on my shoulder, where he would sit up on his hind legs and investigate my ear, in the hope that I had been sensible enough to secrete a palm nut or some other delicacy. As long as there were not more than four people about he would behave with the utmost decorum; a crowd, however, filled him with the unholy desire to be chased. At first I thought that a crowd of people worried and frightened him, and so he ran away to try to escape from them. I soon found out that it was nothing of the sort, for if he found his pursuers lagging behind he would stop, sit up on his hind legs, and wait for them to catch up. There was a certain humour in the fact that we had christened the little brute Sweeti-pie (because of his docility and nice nature) before we discovered his vice. The first race organized by Sweeti-pie took place three days after we had arrived at the marquee.

The water supply for the camp was kept in two great petrol drums, which stood near the kitchen. These were filled every day by the convicts from the local prison, a cheerful group of men, clad in spotless white smocks and shorts, who toiled up the hill to camp every morning, carrying brimming kerosene tins of water on their shaven heads. Behind them would walk

a warder in an impressive fawn uniform, his brass buttons flashing in the sun, swinging a short truncheon with a capable air.
The convicts, whose crimes ranged from petty theft to man-
slaughter, went about their tedious task with great good
humour, and when you greeted them they would all beam with
pleasure. Once a week I distributed a couple of packets of cigarettes among them, and they would be allowed by their warder
(who was having a glass of beer with me) to wander round the
camp and look at our collection of animals. They thoroughly
enjoyed this break in routine, and they would cluster round
the monkeys and double up with laughter at their antics, or
peer into the snake box.

On this particular morning I was on my way to feed Sweeti-
pie when the convicts arrived. They filed past me, their faces
gleaming with sweat, grinning amicably and greeting me with
"Morning, Masa, we done come . . . we done bring water for
Masa . . . Iseeya, Masa . . . " and so on. The warder gave
me a frightfully military salute and then grinned like a small
boy. While they were emptying the contents of their tins into
the petrol drums I got Sweeti-pie out of his cage, sat him on
the palm of my hand, and gave him a lump of sugar to eat.
Glancing round, he saw the group of convicts near the kitchen,
exchanging gossip and saucy badinage with the staff. Having
made sure that there were enough people to give him a good
run for his money, he took a firmer grip on his sugar lump,
leaped lightly off my hand, and galloped off across the camp
clearing, his tail streaming out behind him like a flame in a
draught. I set off in pursuit, but before I had gone more than
a few paces Sweeti-pie had gained the thick bushes at the edge
of the clearing and dived out of sight. Thinking that it would

SWEETI-PIE, BLACK-EARED SQUIRREL

be the last I should see of him, I uttered such a wail of anguish
that everyone dropped what he was doing and ran towards
me.

"Dat beef done run," I yelled to the convicts. "I go pay five
shillings to man who catch um."

The convicts dropped their kerosene tins and rushed off into
the bushes, closely followed by their warder, who discarded
both truncheon and hat, in case they hampered his movements.
The entire staff also joined in the hunt, and the whole crowd
of them went crashing through the bushes and short undergrowth in search of Sweeti-pie. They combed the area thoroughly without finding any sign of the animal, and then it was

discovered that the little brute had been sitting in the branches of a small bush, watching the search sweep to and fro around him, quietly finishing off his sugar lump. When he saw that he'd been spotted he leaped to the ground, ran through the camp clearing and out onto the path leading away over the hill, hotly pursued by a panting mob. Warder, convicts, and staff disappeared from view over the skyline, and peace descended on the camp. But not for long, for in a few minutes Sweeti-pie appeared again over the brow of the hill, galloped down into camp, shot through the marquee, and scrambled into his cage, where he started to eat a piece of sugar cane in the most innocent manner.

Half an hour later the pursuers straggled back to camp, hot and perspiring, to report that the animal had escaped them and was now doubtless deep in the bush. When I showed them Sweeti-pie, who had now finished his meal and was quietly sleeping, and told them how he had returned, they gaped at me for a minute in amazement. And then, being Africans, the humour of the situation struck them and they reeled round the camp, yelling with laughter, slapping their thighs, tears streaming down their faces. The warder was so overcome that he collapsed on the neck of one of the convicts and sobbed with mirth. Every day, after that, the warder and the convicts would bring some offering to the beef that had made them run so fast and "fooled them too much"—a bit of sugar cane, a handful of groundnuts, a bit of cassava, or a piece of bread. Whatever it was, Sweeti-pie would sit up at the wire and receive the offering with squeaks of pleasure, while the convicts would gather round and relate to one another, or to any new member of their group, the story of the squirrel's escapade. Then there would

be much laughter, and Sweeti-pie would be praised for his skil-
ful outflanking tactics. This was only the first of many occasions when Sweeti-pie caused havoc in the camp.

Of the many different creatures that were brought to us
while we were at base camp, about twenty per cent were babies,
and, although these were charming for the most part, they
caused a great deal of extra work, for very young animals require just as much care and attention as a human baby. All these
young creatures endeared themselves to us, but one of the most
charming, and irritating, trio of beasts we acquired were three
little fellows we called the Bandits. These animals were
kusimansels, a kind of mongoose that is fairly common in the
forest. When adult, they are about the size of a large guinea pig,
clad in thick, coarse chocolate-coloured fur, with bushy tails
and long pointed faces with rubbery pink noses and circular,
protuberant boot-button eyes. The Bandits, when they arrived,
were about the size of a small rat and had only just got their
eyes open. Their fur was a bright gingery colour, and it stuck
up in tufts and sprigs all over their bodies, making them look
rather like hedgehogs. Their noses, long and bright pink in colour, were the most prominent part of their anatomy, so flexible
they could be wiffled from side to side, like a miniature elephant's trunk.

At first they had to be fed on milk mixed with calcium and
cod-liver oil, and this was no easy task. They drank more milk
than any other baby animal I have ever met, and the whole business was made more difficult by the fact that they were far too
small to suck it out of the feeding bottle. They had to be fed
by wrapping a lump of cotton wool round a stick, dipping this
in the milk, and then letting them suck it. This worked admi-

rably until their sharp little teeth began to appear through the gums. They were so greedy that they would take hold of the cotton wool and hang like bulldogs, refusing to let go and allow me to dip it into the milk again. On many occasions they would grip so hard that the cotton wool would come off the end of the stick, and then they would try to swallow it; only by sticking my finger down their throats and capturing the cotton wool as it was disappearing could I save them from being choked to death. Sticking a finger down their throats always made them sick, and, of course, as soon as they had been sick they would feel hungry again, and the whole performance would have to be repeated. Anyone who prides himself on his patience should try hand-rearing some baby kusimansels.

As soon as their teeth had come through and they had learned to walk really well, they became most inquisitive and were always trying to push their pink noses into someone else's business. They lived in what we called the nursery, a collection of baskets housing all the baby animals, which were placed between our two beds within easy reach for any bottle feeds that had to be given at night. The top of the basket the Bandits inhabited was not too secure, and it was not long before they learned how to push it off; then they would scramble out and go on a tour of inspection. This was extremely worrisome, for the Bandits seemed to be completely lacking in fear and with equal freedom would stick their noses into monkey cages or snake boxes. Their lives were devoted to a search for food, and everything they came across they would bite, in the hope that it would turn out to be something tasty. At that time we had a fully grown female Colobus monkey, a creature with a wonderfully long thick coat of silky black and white hair, and a

COLOBUS MONKEY AND KUSIMANSELS

long plumelike tail, also black and white, of which she seemed
very proud, for she was always most particular about keeping
it clean and glossy. One day the Bandits escaped from the nursery and wandered round by the monkey cages to see what they
could pick up. The Colobus was reclining on the bottom of her
cage, having a sunbath, and her long beautiful tail was sticking
out between the bars of her cage and lying on the ground. One
of the Bandits discovered this curious black and white object,
and, since it did not appear to belong to anyone, he rushed at it
and sank his sharp little teeth into it to see if it was edible. The
other two, seeing what he had found, immediately joined him.
The unfortunate monkey, screaming with rage and fright,
scrambled to the top of her cage, but this did not shake off the
Bandits. They held on like a vice, and the higher the Colobus
climbed, the higher her tail lifted the Bandits off the ground.
When I arrived on the scene they were suspended about a foot
in the air, revolving slowly, growling through clenched teeth.
It took me several minutes to get them to let go, and then they
did so only because I blew cigarette smoke into their faces and
made them cough.

When the Bandits became old enough to have a special cage
of their own, complete with bedroom, feeding them was a job
fraught with difficulty and danger. They grew so excited at
mealtimes that they would fasten their teeth into anything that
looked even remotely like food, and you had to watch out for
your hands. Instead of waiting until the food dish was put inside their cage, as any sensible animal did, they would leap
through the door to meet it, knock the dish out of your hand,
and then fall to the ground in a tangled heap, screaming loudly
with frustrated rage. I became rather tired of having the Bandits

shoot out like ginger rockets every time I went to feed them, and I evolved a plan. Two of us would approach the cage at mealtimes, and the Bandits would hurl themselves at the bar, screaming loudly, their eyes popping with emotion. One of us would rattle the bedroom door, and they, thinking that the food was being put in there, would throw themselves into the sleeping quarters, fighting and scrambling, for each wanted to get there first. While they were thus engaged you had exactly two seconds' grace before they found out the deception. During that time you had to open the cage door, put the food inside, withdraw your hand, and lock the door again. If you were not quick, or made some slight noise to attract their attention, the Bandits would tumble out of the bedroom, screeching and chittering, upset the plate, and bite indiscriminately at the food and your hand. It was all very trying.

About this time another pair of babies were brought to us, who proved to be full of charm and personality. They were baby red river hogs, and, as with the kusimansels, they looked totally unlike the adult. A fully grown red river hog is probably the most attractive member of the pig family, and certainly the most highly coloured. They have bright rusty-orange coloured fur, with deeper, almost chocolate-coloured markings round the snout. Their large ears end in two extraordinary pencil-like tufts of pure white hair, and a mane of this white hair runs along their backs. The two babies were, like all young pigs, striped: the ground colour was a deep brown, almost black, and from snout to tail they were banded with wide lines of bright mustard-yellow fur, a colour scheme that made them look more like fat wasps than baby pigs.

The little male was the first to arrive, sitting forlornly in a basket carried on the head of a brawny hunter. He was obviously in need of a good feed of warm milk, and as soon as I had paid for him I prepared a bottle and lifted him out onto my knee. He was about the size of a Pekinese and had very sharp little hoofs and tusks, as I soon found out. He treated the feeding bottle with the gravest suspicion at the start. When I tried to get the nipple into his mouth, he kicked and squealed, ripping my trousers with his hoofs and trying to bite with his tiny tusks. At the end of five minutes we both looked as though we had bathed in milk, but not a drop of it had gone down his throat. In the end I had to hold him firmly between my knees, wedge his mouth open with one hand, and squirt milk in with the other. As soon as the first few drops trickled down his throat he stopped struggling and screaming, and within a few minutes he was sucking away at the bottle as hard as he could. After this he was no more trouble, and within two days had lost all his fear of me and would come running to the bars of his pen when I appeared, squeaking and grunting with delight, rolling over on his back to have his bulging stomach scratched.

The female piglet arrived a week later, and she was brought in protesting so loudly that we could hear her long before she and the hunter came in sight. She was almost twice the size of the male, and I decided they must have separate cages to start with, as I thought she might hurt him. But when I put her in the pen next door to him, their obvious delight at seeing each other, and the way they rushed to the intervening bars, squeaking and rubbing noses, made me decide they should share a cage straight away. When I put them in together the tiny male ran forward, sniffing loudly, and then butted the female gently in the ribs; she snorted and skipped away across the cage. He chased her, and together they ran round and round the cage, twisting and turning and doubling back with astonishing agility for such portly beasts. When they had worked off their high spirits they burrowed deep into the pile of dry banana leaves and fell asleep, snoring like a beehive on a summer night.

The little female, being so much older, very soon learned to supplement her bottle feed with a dish of chopped fruit and vegetables. After giving both of them their bottle, I would put a broad, shallow pan full of this mixture into the cage, and she would spend the morning standing there with her nose buried in it, making slushy, squelching noises, and sighing dreamily at intervals. The little male could not understand this and would grow incensed at being ignored; he would prod her with his snout or nibble at her legs until she would suddenly turn on him with squeals of rage and drive him away. He tried several times to see what it was in the dish that attracted her but could not discover anything very exciting about a lot of chopped fruit, so he would wander off moodily and sit in a corner by himself until she had finished. One day, however, he decided that he too could get an extra meal by the simple expedient of sucking the female's long tail. He became convinced that if he sucked long enough and hard enough he would get milk from it. So she would stand there with her nose buried in the dish of food, while behind her stood the male with her tail held hopefully in his mouth. This did not seem to worry her unduly, but he sucked so enthusiastically that her tail became quite bald, and in order to let the hair grow again I had to keep them in separate cages, only letting them be with each other for a game twice a day.

Life in the marquee with half a hundred animals to look after was anything but dull. We were surrounded by animals of all shapes and sizes and kinds, from tree frogs to owls, from pythons to monkeys. At all hours of the day and night a steady mutter of strange noises filled the air, ranging from the maniacal screams and giggles of the chimpanzees to the steady rasping sound of a pouched rat that was convinced he could, by sticking to it in spite of all opposition, gnaw his way through a metal feeding pot. At any time of the day you could find something to do or something new to note or observe. The following quotations from a week's entries in my diary give some indication of the wealth of small but exciting or interesting incidents.

"The young female Stanger's squirrels' eyes have now changed from that beautiful shade of sky blue to steel grey; when you disturb her at night she makes a noise like a clockwork train when it is lifted off the rails. . . . One of the palm vipers has given birth to eleven young: about five inches long, ground colour pale slate grey with cross bands of dark ash grey, making wonderful contrast to vivid green and white mother; they all struck viciously at a stick when only a couple of hours old. . . . Large green tree frogs make a noise like a clock slowly ticking, just before rain, but will stop if you go near their cage and won't perform again until the next cloudburst. . . . Discovered that the galagos like the flowers of a species of marigold that grows around here; they hold flower head in one hand and pluck off petals with the other, cramming them into their mouths; then they play with the remains as though it were a shuttlecock, looking quite ridiculous, with their great eyes staring. . . .

"Feeding notes: Golden cat adores brain and liver chopped
up and mixed with raw egg—exotic tastes some of these beasts
have! Pangolins (scaly anteaters) won't eat their egg and milk
mixture if it's sweetened but simply overturn dish—extremely
annoying! Fruit bats prefer their bananas to be given with the
skins on; they eat the whole lot, and the skin seems to prevent
their bowels from becoming too loose. Overripe fruit causes
havoc among the monkey bowels (especially chimps—messy!),
yet the bats will eat and enjoy without ill effects fruit that is
fermenting, providing there is roughage with it. Too much
goat meat causes rupture of the anus in the marsh mongooses,
for some peculiar reason; warm cod-liver oil and very gentle
pressure will get it back into place; animal will become very
exhausted and then one drop whisky in tablespoon of water
helps them."

These were the little things that made up life in base camp,
but they were of absorbing interest to us, and the days seemed
so full of colour and incident that they sped past unnoticed.
So it is not surprising that I was rather terse with a pleasant but
rather stupid young man who said, after being shown round
the collection, "Don't you ever go out and have a pot at a monkey or something? Should have thought you'd have died of
boredom, stuck down here all day with this lot."

II.   THE FOREST OF FLYING MICE

When I returned from the mountains to our Cross River base
camp there was only one gap of importance in our collection.
The gap was noticeable to me, for it was caused by the absence
of a tiny animal I was most anxious to catch. The English name
for this beast is the pigmy scaly-tail, while zoologists, in their
usual flippant and familiar manner, call it *Idiurus kivuensis*.
When in England I had pored over drawings and museum
skins of the beast, and since our arrival in Africa I had talked
about it incessantly, until even the staff knew that *Idiurus kivuensis* was the name of a beef that I prized beyond all measure.

I knew that *Idiurus* was a strictly nocturnal animal, and since
it was only the size of a small mouse I thought it unlikely that
any of the hunters would know it. I was right, for they did not
recognize the drawing. From the small amount of literature in

existence dealing with the species I had managed to glean the fact that they lived in colonies in hollow trees, preferring the less accessible portions of the forest. I explained this to the hunters, in the faint hope that it would spur them on to search for specimens, but it was no use; the African will not hunt for an animal he has never seen, for he considers it possible that it may not exist, and so to hunt for it would be a waste of time. I had precisely the same trouble over the hairy frogs, and so I realized that my tales of small small rats that flew like birds from tree to tree was doomed from the start. One thing was very clear: if I wanted *Idiurus* I would have to go out and hunt for it myself, and I should have to do so quickly, for our time was short. I decided to make the village of Eshobi my head-quarters for the hunt. It was a day's march from base camp, in the depths of the forest, and I knew the inhabitants well, for I had stayed there on a previous visit to the Cameroons. Hunting for a creature the size of a mouse in the deep rain forest that stretches for several hundred miles in all directions may sound like an improved version of the needle-in-the-haystack routine, but it is this sort of thing that makes collecting so interesting. My chances of success were one in a thousand, but I set off cheerfully into the forest.

The Eshobi road can be appreciated only by someone who possesses a saintlike predilection for mortifying the flesh. Most of it resembles an old dried watercourse, though it follows a route that no self-respecting river would take. It moves in a series of erratic zigzags through the trees, occasionally running down a steep slope into a valley, crossing a small stream, and climbing up the opposite side. On the downward slope the rocks and stones that make up its surface are always loose, so that on occasions your descent is quicker than you anticipated. However, as the road starts to climb up the opposite side of the valley, you find that the rocks have increased considerably in size and are placed like a series of steps. This is a snare and a delusion, for each rock has been so cunningly placed that it is quite impossible to step from one to the other. They are all thickly covered with a cloak of green moss, wild begonias, and ferns, so you cannot tell, before jumping, exactly what shape your landing ground is going to be.

We followed this track for some three miles and then toiled up from the bottom of a deep valley and found that the forest floor was level and the path almost as smooth as a motor road. It wound and twisted its way through the giant trees, and here and there along its length a rent in the foliage above let through a shaft of sunlight. In these patches of sun, warming themselves after the night's dew, sat a host of butterflies. They rose and flew round us as we walked, dipping and fluttering and wheeling in a sun-drunken condition. There were tiny white ones like fragile chips of snow, great clumsy ones whose wings shone like burnished copper, and others decked out in blacks, greens, reds, and yellows. Once we had passed, they settled once more on the sunlit path and sat there gaily, occasionally opening and closing their wings.

This ballet of butterflies is always to be seen on the Eshobi path, and is, moreover, the only life you are likely to see, for the deep forest does not teem with dangerous game, as some books would have you believe.

We followed this path for about three hours, stopping at times so that the sweating carriers could lower their loads to the ground and have a rest. Presently the path curved, and as we rounded a corner the forest ended and we found ourselves walking up the main and only street of Eshobi. Dogs barked, chickens scuttled and squawked out of our way, and a small toddler rose from the dust where he had been playing and fled into the nearest hut, screaming his lungs out. Suddenly, as if from nowhere, we were surrounded by a milling crowd of humanity: men and boys, women of all ages, all grinning and clapping, pushing forward to shake me by the hand.

"Welcome, Masa! Welcome!"

"You done come, Masa!"

"Iseeya, Masa, welcome!"

"Eh-aehh! Masa, you done come back to Eshobi!"

I was escorted down the village street by this welcoming, chattering mob of humanity as though I were royalty. Someone rushed for a chair, and I was seated in state with the entire village standing admiringly round me, beaming and ejaculating "welcome" at intervals, now and again clapping their hands or cracking their knuckles in an excess of delight.

I was still greeting old friends and inquiring after people's relatives and offspring when my carriers and the cook appeared. A long argument ensued as to where I should stay, and at last the villagers decided that the only place fit for such a distinguished visitor was their newly built dance hall. This was a large circular hut, the floor of which had been worn to the smoothness of planed wood by the trampling and shuffling of hundreds of feet. The drums, flutes, and rattles were hastily removed, the floor was swept, and I was installed.

After I had eaten and drunk, the village gathered round once again to hear what I had come for this time. I explained at great length that I had come only for a short visit and wanted only one kind of creature, and I went on to describe *Idiurus*. I showed them a drawing of the animal, and it was passed from hand to hand, and everyone shook his head over it and said sorrowfully he had never seen it. My heart sank.

I picked out three hunters with whom I had worked before. I told them that they were to go to the forest immediately, find all the hollow trees they could, and mark them. On the following day they were to come tell me what success they had met with and guide me to the trees. Then I asked if there was anyone present who could climb trees. A dozen or so hands went up. The volunteers were a very mixed crowd, and I eyed them doubtfully.

"You fit climb stick?" I asked.

"Yes, sah, we fit," came the instant but untruthful chorus.

I pointed to an enormous tree that grew at the edge of the village. "You fit climb dat big stick?"

Immediately the number of volunteers dwindled, until at last only one man still had his hand up.

"You fit climb dat big stick?" I repeated, thinking he had not heard.

"Yes, sah," he said.

"For true?"

"Yes, sah, I fit climb um. I fit climb stick big pass dat one."

"All right. You go come for bush with me tomorrow, you hear?"

"Yes, sah," said the man, grinning.

"Na what they de call you?"

"Peter, sah."

"Right. You go come tomorrow for early early morning time."

The hunters and the other village inhabitants dispersed, and I unpacked my equipment and made ready for the next day.

That evening the entire village returned silently and cautiously, to watch me have my bath. This they were able to do in comparative comfort, for the walls of the dance hall had many windows and cracks. There must have been some fifty people watching me as I covered myself with soap, singing lustily the while, but I did not become aware of the fact for quite some time. It did not worry me, for I am not unduly modest, and as long as my audience (fifty per cent of which consisted of women) was silent and made no ribald remarks I was content that they should watch. However, Jacob arrived at that moment and was shocked beyond belief at the disgusting inquisitiveness of the villagers. Seizing a stick, he dashed at them and drove them away in a rushing, screaming mob. He returned panting and full of righteous indignation. Soon afterwards I discovered that he had overlooked two of the crowd, for their earnest black faces were wedged in one of the windows.

I called Jacob. "They done come back," I said, waving a soapy hand at the window.

He examined the faces. "No, sah," he said seriously, "dis one na my friends."

Apparently I was not to be defiled by being watched by an indiscriminate mass of villagers, but any personal friends of Jacob's were in a different category. It was not until later that I learned that Jacob was something of a businessman: after driving away the crowd he had announced that those who would pay him a penny for the privilege of watching me

bathe would be allowed to return. He did quite a brisk trade
among the younger members of the village, many of whom had
never seen a European and who wanted to settle various bets
as to whether or not I was white all over.

Very early the next morning my hunters and my tree
climber appeared. The hunters, it turned out, had found and
marked some thirty trees, but these were dispersed over such
a wide area of the forest that it would be impossible to visit
them all in one day. I decided to start with the farthest ones and
gradually work back towards the village.

The path we followed was a typical bush path, about eighteen inches wide, that coiled and twisted among the trees like
a dying snake. At first it led up an extremely steep hillside,
through massive boulders, each topped with a patch of ferns
and moss and starred with the flowers of a tiny pink primrose-
like plant. Here and there the great lianas coiled down from the
trees and lay across our path in strange shapes, curving and
twisting like giant pythons. At the top of this steep incline
the path flattened out and ran across the level forest floor between the great tree trunks.

The interior of the forest is cool, and the light is dim. Flickering as it does through the dense fretwork of leaves, it possesses a curious underwater quality. The forest is not the tangled mass of undergrowth that you read about: it is composed
of the enormous pillarlike trunks of the trees, set well apart
and interspersed with thin undergrowth, young saplings and
low-growing plants that lurk in the semigloom.

We travelled onwards, following the faint trail, for some
four miles before one of the hunters stopped and stuck his
cutlass into the trunk of a tree with a ringing "chunk."

"Dis na tree dat get hole for inside, sah," he announced.

At the base of the trunk was a longitudinal slit, some two feet wide and three feet high. I bent and stuck my head inside and then twisted round so that I could look up the tree. But if there was a top opening it was hidden from me by some twist of the trunk, for no light filtered down from above. I sniffed vigorously, but all I could smell was rotting wood. The base of the tree yielded nothing but a few bat droppings and the dried husks of various insects. It did not look to be a particularly good tree, but I thought we might as well try smoking it out to see what it contained.

Smoking out a big forest tree, when it is done occasionally, is a thrilling procedure. During my search for *Idiurus* the thrill rather wore off, but this was because we were forced to smoke so many trees a day, and a great proportion of these proved to have nothing whatsoever inside them. The smoking of a tree is quite an art and requires a certain amount of practice before you can perfect it. First, having found your tree and made sure that it is really hollow all the way up, you have to make sure whether there are any exit holes farther up the trunk, and if there are, you have to send a man up to cover them with nets. Having done this, you drape a net over the main hole at the base of the tree, and this has to be done in such a way that it does not interfere with the smoking process and yet prevents anything from getting away. The important thing is to make sure that this net is secure: there is nothing quite so exasperating as to have it fall down and envelop you in its folds just as the creatures inside the tree are starting to come out. With all your nets in position you have to deal with the problem of the fire: this, contrary to all proverbial expectations, has to be all smoke and no fire, unless you want your specimens roasted. A small pile of dry twigs is laid in the opening, soaked with kerosene, and set alight. As soon as it is ablaze, you lay a handful of green leaves on top, and keep replenishing them. The burning of these green leaves produces scarcely any flame but vast quantities of pungent smoke, which is immediately sucked up into the hollow interior of the tree. Your next problem is to make sure that there is not too much smoke, for, if you are not careful, you can quite easily asphyxiate your specimens before they can rush out of the tree. The idea is to strike the happy medium between roasting and suffocation. Once the fire has been lit and piled with green leaves, it generally takes about three minutes (depending on the size of the tree) before the smoke percolates to every part and the animals start to break cover.

We smoked our first tree, and all we got out of it was an indignant moth. We took down the nets, put out the fire, and continued on our way. The next marked tree was half a mile away, and when we reached it we went through the same procedure. This time it was slightly more exciting, for, although there were no *Idiurus* in the trunk, there was some life: the first thing to break cover was a small gecko, beautifully banded in chocolate and ash grey. These little lizards are quite plentiful in the deep forest, and you generally find two or three in any hollow tree you smoke. Following hard on the gecko's tail came three creatures that looked, as they crawled hastily out of the smoke, like large brown sausages with a fringe of undulating legs along each side: they were giant millipedes, large, stupid, and completely harmless insects common all over the forest. The hollow interior of trees is their favourite

abode, for their diet is rotten wood. This, it seemed, was the
entire contents of the tree. We took down the nets, put out the
fire, and went on. The next tree was completely empty, as were
the three that followed it. The seventh tree produced a small
colony of bats, all of which flew frantically out of a hole at
the top as soon as Peter tried to climb the tree.

The laborious process of setting up the nets, smoking the
tree, taking down the nets, and moving on to the next tree was
repeated fifteen times that day, and towards evening we were
sore and smarting from a thousand cuts and bruises, and our
throats were rough with breathing in lungfuls of smoke. We
were all in the deepest depths of depression, for not only had
we not caught any *Idiurus*, but we had caught nothing else
of any value either. By the time we reached the last tree that
we would have time to smoke before it got dark I was so tired
I didn't care whether there were any *Idiurus* in the trunk or
not. I squatted on the ground, smoking a cigarette, and watched
the hunters as they made the preparations. The tree was
smoked, and nothing whatsoever appeared from inside. The
hunters looked at me.

"Take down the nets. We go back for Eshobi," I said
wearily.

Jacob was busily disentangling the net from the trunk when
he paused and peered at something that lay inside the tree.
He bent, picked it up, and came over to me. "Masa want dis
kind of beef?" he inquired diffidently.

I glanced up, and received a considerable shock, for there,
dangling from his fingers by its long feathery tail, its eyes
closed and its sides heaving, was an *Idiurus*. He deposited the

IDIURUS

mouse-sized creature in my cupped hands, and I peered at it: it was quite unconscious, apparently almost asphyxiated by the smoke.

"Quick, quick, Jacob!" I cried, in an agony of fear. "Bring me small box for put um—no, no, not that one, a good one. Now put small leaf for inside—*small leaf*, you moron, not half a tree. There, that's right."

I placed the *Idiurus* reverently inside the box and took another look at it. It lay there quite limp and unconscious, its chest heaving and its tiny pink paws twitching. It looked to be on the verge of death; frantically seizing a huge bunch of leaves, I fanned it vigorously. A quarter of an hour of this peculiar form of artificial respiration and, to my delight, the animal started to recover. Its eyes opened blearily, it rolled onto its stomach and lay there looking miserable. I fanned a while longer, then carefully closed the lid of the box.

While I had been trying to revive the *Idiurus* the hunters

had been grouped round me in a silent, sorrowful circle; now that they saw the creature regain its faculties, they gave me broad grins of delight. We hastily conducted a search of the interior of the tree, to see if there were any more lying about, but we found nothing. This puzzled me considerably, for *Idiurus* was supposed to live in large colonies. To find a solitary one, therefore, was unusual. I sincerely hoped that the text-books were not wrong; to catch some specimens from a colony of animals is infinitely easier than trying to track down and capture solitary individuals. However, I could not stop to worry about it; I wanted to get the precious creature back to the village and out of the small travelling box it was in. We packed up the nets and set off through the twilit forest as speedily as we could. I carried the box in my cupped hands as delicately as if it contained eggs, and at intervals I would fan the creature through the wire-gauze top.

When I was safely back in the village dance hall I prepared a larger cage and moved the beast into it. This was not so easy, for it had fully recovered from the smoke by now and scuttled about with considerable speed. At last, without letting it escape, or getting bitten, I succeeded in manoeuvring it into the new cage. I placed my strongest light next to the cage in order to have a good look.

The creature was approximately the size of a common house mouse and very similar in general shape. The first thing that caught my attention was the tail: it was very long (almost twice as long as the body) and down each side grew a fringe of long wavy hairs, giving the whole tail the appearance of a rather bedraggled feather. The head was large and rather domed, with small, pixie-pointed ears. The eyes were pitch-black, small and rather prominent. The rodent teeth, a pair of large bright orange-coloured incisors, protruded from the mouth in a gentle curve, so that from the side it had an extraordinarily supercilious expression. Perhaps the most curious part was the "flying" membrane, a long fine flap of skin, stretching along each side of the body, and attached to the ankles and to a long slightly curved cartilaginous shaft growing out from the arm, just behind the elbow. When the animal was at rest, the membrane was curled and folded along the side of its body like a curtain; when it launched itself into the air, however, the legs were stretched out straight and the membrane drawn taut, acting like the wings of a glider. Later I was to discover just how skillful *Idiurus* could be in the air, in spite of this rather primitive gliding apparatus.

When I had gone to bed that night and switched off the light I could hear my new specimen rustling and scuttling round the cage, and I imagined what a feast it was having on the variety of foods I had put in there. But when dawn came and I crawled sleepily out of bed to have a look, I discovered nothing had been eaten. I was not unduly worried, for some creatures when newly caught refuse to eat until they have settled down in captivity. The length of time this takes varies not only with the species but with the individual animal. I felt that sometime during the day *Idiurus* would come down from the top of the cage where it was clinging and eat its fill.

When the hunters arrived we set out through the mist-whitened forest to a fresh series of trees. Refreshed by a night's sleep and by our capture of the day before, we went about the laborious smoking process with a great deal more enthusiasm. But by midday we had investigated ten trees and found noth-

ing. We had by this time reached a section of the forest where
the trees were enormous even for the West African forest.
They stood well apart, but even so their massive branches
interlocked above. The trunks, which in most cases were at
least fifteen feet in diameter, had great buttress roots growing
out from their bases like supporting walls of a cathedral, each
well over ten feet high where it joined the trunk, and with a
space of a good-sized room between each flange. Some of them
had massive, muscular-looking creepers as thick as my body
wound round them. We made our way through the giant
trunks and came presently to a dip in the level forest floor,
a small dell in which stood one of these enormous trees more or
less by itself.

At the edge of the dell the hunters paused and pointed.
"Na dis big stick get hole too much, sah," they chorused.

We approached the trunk of the tree, and between two of
the flanges I saw a huge arched rent in the wood about the size
and shape of a small church door. I paused at the entrance and
looked up: the tree trunk towered above me, shooting up
smooth and branchless towards the sky for about two hundred
feet. Not a stump, not a branch, broke the smooth surface of
that column of wood. I began to hope that there would be
nothing inside the tree, for I could not see for the life of me
how anyone was going to climb up to the top and put nets over
the exit holes, if any. I walked into the hollow interior of the
tree as I would walk into a room, and there was plenty of space;
the sunlight filtered gently in through the entrance, and gradually my eyes became accustomed to the dim light. I peered
upwards, but a slight bend in the trunk prevented my seeing
very far. I tested the sides of the tree and found them composed

of rotten wood, soft and spongy. By kicking with my toes I found it was quite easy to make footholds, and I laboriously climbed up the inside of the trunk until I was high enough to crane round the corner. The trunk stretched up as hollow as a factory chimney, and just as big. At the very summit of the tree there was a large exit hole, and through it poured a shaft of sunlight. Suddenly I nearly released my rather precarious hold with excitement, for I saw that the top part of the trunk was literally a moving carpet of *Idiurus*. They slid about on the rotten wood as swiftly and silently as shadows, and when they were still they disappeared completely from sight, so perfectly did they match the background. I slid to the ground and made my way out into the open.

The hunters looked at me expectantly. "Na beef for inside, Masa?" asked one.

"Yes. Na plenty beef for inside. You go look."

Chattering excitedly, they pushed into the interior of the tree. Some idea of its size may be gained from the fact that Peter, Jacob, and the three hunters could all fit comfortably into its spacious interior. I could hear their ejaculations of astonishment as they saw the animals, and sharp words being exchanged when someone (I suspected Jacob) trod on somebody else's face in his excitement.

I walked slowly round the tree, searching the trunk for any footholds or handholds on the bark which would enable Peter to climb to the top, but the bark was as smooth as a billiard ball. The tree seemed unclimbable, and I damped the hunters' gaiety by pointing this out when they emerged from the trunk. While we all sat on the ground and smoked and discussed the matter, Jacob prowled round the dell, scowling ferociously

at the trees, and presently he came over to us and said he
thought he had found a way for Peter to get up to the top.
We followed him across the dell to its extreme edge, where he
pointed to a tall thin sapling whose top just reached one of
the great branches of the main tree. Jacob suggested that Peter
shin up the sapling, get on the branch, and work his way along
it until he reached the top of the hollow trunk.

Peter examined the sapling suspiciously but said he would
try. He spat on his hands, seized the trunk of the sapling, and
climbed aloft, using his almost prehensile toes to get extra grip
against the bark. When he reached the halfway mark, however,
some seventy feet from the ground, his weight started to bend
the sapling over like a bow, and before he had gone much
farther the trunk was creaking ominously. It was obvious that
the tree was too slender to support the weight of my corpulent
tree climber, and he was forced to return to earth.

Jacob, grinning excitedly, came strutting across to where
I stood. "Masa, I fit climb dat stick," he said. "I no be fat man
like Peter."

"Fat!" said Peter indignantly. "Who you de call fat, eh?
I no be fat. Dat stick no get power for hold man, dats all."

"You be fat," said Jacob scornfully. "All time you fill your
belly with food, an' now Masa want you to climb stick you no
fit."

"All right, all right," I said hastily. "You go try and climb,
Jacob. But take care you no go fall, eh?"

"Yes, sah," he said. He ran to the sapling, flung himself onto
the trunk, and went up it like a caterpillar.

Jacob weighed about half as much as Peter, and he was soon
clinging to the very tip of the sapling, and the tree was still

upright, though it swayed round and round in a gentle curve.
Each time it passed the branch of the big tree Jacob made a
wild grab—and missed. He looked down. "Masa, I no fit
catch um," he called.

"All right, come down," I shouted back. He descended
rapidly to the ground, and I gave him the end of a long length
of strong cord. "You go tie dis for top, eh? Den, when you
ready, we go pull dis small stick so it come for dis big one.
Understand?"

"Yes, sah," said Jacob gleefully and scuttled up the sapling
again.

When he reached the top he fastened the rope round the
sapling and shouted down that he was ready. We laid hold of
the rope and pulled lustily. As we backed slowly across the
clearing, digging our toes into the soft leaf mould to gain a
grip, the sapling bent slowly over until its tip touched the great
branch. Quickly Jacob reached out, got a grip on the branch,
and hauled himself across. We held on to the sapling until he
had pulled a piece of rope from out of his loincloth and tied
the top of it to the branch on which he was now lying. When
the sapling was tied we released our hold on the rope gently.

Jacob was standing upright on the branch now, holding on
to the smaller growth that sprouted from it, and he slowly
moved along towards the main trunk, walking warily, for the
branch he was using as a road was thickly overgrown with
orchids, creepers, and tree ferns, an ideal habitat for a tree
snake. When he reached the place where the branch joined
the tree he sat astride it and lowered a long piece of string.
To the end of this we tied a bundle of nets and some small
boxes in which to put any specimens he caught at the top. With

these safely tied round his waist he moved round the tree to the hole, which was situated in the crotch where the great branches spread away from the trunk. Squatting down, he spread the net over the hole and arranged the boxes within easy reach.

"All right, Masa, your hunter man 'e ready now," he shouted, grinning down at us mischievously.

"Hunter man!" muttered Peter. "Dis cook call himself hunter man—eh-aehh!"

We collected a mass of dry twigs and green leaves and laid the fire in the great chimneylike opening of the tree. We lit it and piled the green leaves on, after draping a net over the arched opening. The fire smouldered sullenly for a few minutes, and then the frail wisp of smoke grew stronger, and soon a great stream of grey smoke was pouring up the hollow shell of the tree.

Jacob, perched precariously, was peering down into the interior of the trunk when the thick column of grey smoke swept up and enveloped him. We could hear him coughing and choking and could see him moving round gingerly in the smoke, in an effort to find a more suitable spot to sit. It seemed to me, waiting excitedly, that the *Idiurus* took a tremendously long time to be affected by the smoke. I was just wondering if perhaps they had all been knocked unconscious before they could attempt to escape when the first one broke cover. It scuttled out of the opening in the base of the tree and tried to launch itself into the air, but immediately became tangled up in the nets. One of the hunters rushed forward to disentangle it, but before I could go help him the entire colony decided to vacate the tree in a body. Numbers of *Idiurus* appeared at the main opening and leaped into the net. I discovered to my annoyance

that there were two or three cracks in the trunk, some thirty
feet above the ground, which we had overlooked, and through
these minute openings the *Idiurus* were swarming out into the
open air. They scuttled about the bark and seemed quite un-
perturbed by either the strong sunlight or our presence, for
some of them came down to within six feet of the ground.
They moved with incredible rapidity over the surface of the
wood, seeming more to glide than run. Then an extra large,
pungent cloud of smoke burst upwards and spread over them,
and they decided to take to the air.

I have seen some extraordinary sights at one time and another, but the flight of the flying mice I shall remember until
my dying day. The great tree was encircled by shifting col-
umns of grey smoke that turned to the most ethereal blue where
the great bars of sunlight stabbed through it. Into this the
Idiurus launched themselves. They left the trunk of the tree
without any apparent effort; one minute they were clinging
spread-eagled to the bark, the next they were in the air. Their
tiny legs were stretched out, and the membranes along their
sides were taut. They swooped and drifted through the tumbling clouds of smoke with all the assurance and skill of hawking swallows, twisting and banking with incredible skill and
little or no movement of the body. This was pure gliding, and
what they achieved with it was astonishing. I saw one leave
the trunk of the tree at a height of about thirty feet. It glided
across the dell in a straight, steady swoop and landed on a tree
about a hundred and fifty feet away, losing little, if any, height
in the process. Others left the trunk of the smoke-enveloped
tree and glided round it in a series of diminishing spirals, to
land on a portion of the trunk lower down. Some patrolled the

IDIURUS IN FLIGHT

tree in a series of S-shaped patterns, doubling back on their tracks with great smoothness and efficiency. Their ability in the air amazed me, for there was no breeze in the forest to set up the air currents I should have thought essential for such intricate manoeuvring.

I noticed that, although a number of them had flown off into the forest, the majority stayed on the main trunk, contenting themselves with taking short flights round it when the smoke got too severe. This gave me an idea. I put out the fire, and as the smoke gradually drifted and dispersed the *Idiurus* that were on the tree all scuttled back inside. We gave them a few minutes to settle down, while I examined the ones we had caught. At the base of the tree we had captured eight females and four males. Jacob lowered his catch down from the smoke-filled heavens, and it consisted of two males and one female. With them were two of the most extraordinary bats I have ever seen, with golden-brown backs, bright lemon-yellow shirtfronts, faces like pigs, and long piglike ears that twisted down over their noses.

When the *Idiurus* had all returned to the interior we relit the fire, and once again they all rushed out. This time, however, they had grown wise, and the majority refused to come anywhere near the nets at the main opening. Jacob had better luck and soon lowered a bag containing five females. This made a total of twenty specimens, which I thought was quite enough. We put out the fire, took down the nets, got Jacob down from his perch—not without some difficulty, for he was very eager to catch the rest of the colony—and then set off through the forest to walk the four-odd miles to the village. I carried the precious bag of *Idiurus*, squeaking and scrambling, carefully in my hands, occasionally stopping to undo the top and fan them, for I was not at all sure they were getting sufficient air through the sides of the fine linen bag.

We reached the village, tired and dirty, just after dark. I put the *Idiurus* in the largest cage I had, but it was far too small for such a great number. Stupidly I had banked on getting only two or three, if I got any at all, and so I had not brought a really large cage with me. I feared that if I left them in that confined space overnight the casualties in the morning would be heavy. There was only one thing to do, and that was to get the precious beasts back to the base camp as quickly as possible. I wrote a brief note to Smith, telling him that I had been successful, and that I would be arriving around midnight with the animals, and would he please have a large cage ready for them. I sent this off at once, then had a bath and some food. I reckoned that my letter would arrive at the camp about an hour before I did, which should give Smith plenty of time to improvise a cage.

About ten o'clock my little party started off along the Eshobi road. First walked Jacob, carrying the lantern. Following him came a carrier with the box of *Idiurus* balanced on his woolly head. I was next in the row, and behind me was another carrier with my bed on his head. The Eshobi path is bad enough in broad daylight; by night it is a death trap. As a source of illumination the lantern was about as much use as an anaemic glowworm; the light it gave was just sufficient to distort everything and to shroud rocks in deep shadow. Our progress was necessarily slow. Normally that walk would have taken us about two hours; it took us five. Most of the way I was on the edge of a nervous breakdown, for the carrier with the

Idiurus hopped and jumped among the rocks like a mountain goat, and every minute I expected to see him slip and my precious box of specimens go hurtling into a ravine. He got more and more daring as the path got worse, until I felt that it was only a matter of time before he fell.

"My friend," I called, "if you go drop my beef, we no go reach Mamfe together. I go bury you here."

He took the hint and slowed his progress considerably.

Halfway across a small stream my shadow got in the way of the carrier behind me. He missed his footing, stumbled, and deposited my bed and bedding into the water with a loud splash. He was very upset, although I pointed out that it was mainly my fault. We continued on our way, the carrier with the dripping load on his head muttering at intervals, "Eh! Sorry, sah," in a doleful voice.

The forest was full of tiny sounds, the faint cracking of twigs, an occasional call from a frightened bird, the steady throbbing cry of the cicadas on the tree trunks, and now and again a shrill piping from a tree frog. The streams we crossed were ice-cold and transparent, and they whispered and licked at the big boulders in a conspiratorial fashion. At one point Jacob, up ahead, let out a loud yelp and started to dance wildly, swinging the lamp so that the shadows writhed and twisted among the tree trunks.

"Na whatee, na whatee?" called the carriers.

"Na ant," said Jacob, still twirling round. "Blurry ant too much."

Not looking where he was going, he had trodden on a column of driver ants crossing the path, a black stream two inches wide that poured from the undergrowth on one side of the path and into the undergrowth on the other side like a steady, silent river of tar. As his foot came down on them the whole line seemed to boil up suddenly and silently, and within a second the ants were swarming over the ground in a horde, spreading farther and farther round the scene of the attack, like an ink stain on the brown leaves. The carriers and I had to make a detour into the forest to avoid their ferocious attentions.

As we left the shelter of the forest and walked out into the first moon-silvered grassfield it started to rain. At first, it was a fine, drifting drizzle, more like mist; then, without warning, the sky let down a seemingly solid deluge of water that bent the grass flat and turned the path into a treacherous slide of red mud. Fearing that my precious box of specimens would get drenched, and the *Idiurus* die in consequence, I took off my coat and draped it over the cage on the carrier's head. It was not much protection, but it helped. We struggled on, up to our ankles in mud, until we came to the river we had to ford. Crossing this took us, I suppose, roughly three minutes, but it was quite long enough, for the carrier with the *Idiurus* on his head stumbled and staggered over the rocky bed, while the current plucked and pushed at him, waiting for an opportunity to catch him off balance. But we arrived intact on the opposite bank, and soon we saw the lights of the camp gleaming through the trees. Just as we got to the marquee the rain stopped.

The cage Smith had prepared was not really large enough, but I felt that the main thing was to get the creatures out of the dripping box as soon as possible. Carefully we undid the door and stood watching with baited breath as the tiny animals scuttled into their new home. None appeared to have got wet, which relieved me, though one or two looked a bit the worse for wear.

"What do they eat?" inquired Smith when we had gloated over them for five minutes.

"I haven't the faintest idea. The one I caught yesterday didn't eat anything, though God knows I gave him enough choice."

"Um, I expect they'll eat when they settle down a bit."

"Oh yes, I think they will," I said cheerfully, and I really believed it.

We filled the cage with every form of food and drink there was to be had in camp, until it looked like a native market. Then we hung a sack over the front of the cage and left the *Idiurus* to eat.

Since my bed had absorbed rain and river water like a sponge, I was forced to spend a most uncomfortable night dozing in an upright camp chair. I slept fitfully until dawn, when I got up and hobbled over to the *Idiurus* cage, lifted the sacking, and peered inside.

On the floor, among the completely untouched food and drink, lay a dead *Idiurus*. The others clung to the top of the cage like a flock of bats and twittered suspiciously at me. I retrieved the dead specimen and carried it over to the table, where I subjected it to a careful dissection. The stomach was crammed with the partially digested red husk of the palm nut. This was the very last thing I expected to find, for the palm nut is, in the Cameroons at any rate, a cultivated product and does not grow wild in the forest. If the rest of the colony had been eating palm nuts the night before they were captured, it meant they must have travelled some four miles to the nearest native farm and then come down to within a few feet of the ground to feed. This was all very puzzling, but it gave me something to work on, and the next night their cage was festooned like a Christmas tree with bunches of red palm nuts, in addition to the other foods. We put the food in at dusk, and for the next three hours Smith and I carried on long conversations that had nothing to do with *Idiurus*, and with an effort we pretended not to hear the squeaks and rustlings that came from their cage. After we had eaten, however, the strain became too great, and we crept up to the cage and gently lifted a corner of the sacking.

The entire colony was down on the floor of the cage, and all of them were busily engaged in eating palm nuts. They squatted on their haunches and held the nuts in their minute pink forepaws like squirrels, turning the nuts quickly as their teeth shredded off the scarlet rind. They stopped eating as we lifted the sacking and peered at us; one or two of the more timid ones dropped their nuts and fled to the top of the cage, but the majority decided we were harmless and continued to eat. We dropped the sacking into place and executed a war dance round the marquee, uttering loud cries to indicate our pleasure, cries that awoke the monkeys and set them chattering a protest, and brought the staff tumbling out of the kitchen to see what was the matter. When they heard the good news that the new beef was chopping at last they grinned and cracked their knuckles with pleasure, for they took our work very much to heart. All day gloom had pervaded the camp because the new beef would not chop, but now everything was all right, and so the staff returned to the kitchen, chattering and laughing.

But our joy was short-lived, for the next morning we found two *Idiurus* dead. From then on our little colony diminished steadily, week by week. They would eat only palm nuts, and, apparently, this was not enough for them. The variety of food they refused was quite astonishing—because even with the most finicky animal you will generally strike something it likes if you offer it a wide enough choice of food. It appeared that the *Idiurus* were not going to be easy to get back to England.

12. A WILDERNESS OF MONKEYS

Perhaps the most noisy, most irritating, and most lovable creatures that shared our marquee were the monkeys. There were forty of them altogether, and life under the same roof with forty monkeys is anything but quiet. The adult animals were not so bad; it was the baby monkeys that caused so much trouble and extra work. They would scream loudly if left alone, demand bottles full of warm wilk at the most ungodly hours of night and morning, get stricken with all sorts of baby complaints, and frighten us to death. They would escape from the nursery and get near the golden cat's cage, or fall into kerosene tins full of water. We were forced to think up the most Machiavellian schemes for dealing with them, and some were quite extraordinary.

Take the case of the baby drills. These baboons are extremely common in the forests of the Cameroons, and we were always being brought babies of all ages. The drill is that rather ugly-looking creature you can see in most zoos, which has a bright pink behind and does not hesitate to share its glory with you. Very young drills are one of the most pathetic and ridiculous-looking creatures in the world: they are covered with very fine silvery-grey fur, and their heads, hands, and feet look at least three times too big for their bodies. The hands, feet, and face are a shade that we used to describe as boiled baby pink, and their minute bottoms are the same colour. The skin on their bodies is white, spotted in places with large areas, exactly like big birthmarks, of bright china blue. Combine all this with the fact that, like all baby monkeys, they have staring eyes and long, attenuated arms and legs that tremble like the limbs of a very old person, and you have some idea of a baby drill.

The early days of a drill's life are spent clinging with its muscular hands and feet to the thick fur of its mother. So our baby drills, when they had transferred their affections to us and decided that we were their parents, demanded loudly and vociferously that they be allowed to cling to us. Next to vast quantities of food, the most important thing in a young drill's life is to feel that it has a good grip on the provider of the food. As it is almost impossible to work when you have four or five baby drills clinging to you like miniature, cackling Old Men of the Sea, we had to devise a plan to keep them

happy. We found two old coats and slung these over the backs
of chairs in the centre of the marquee; then we introduced the
babies to them. They were used to seeing us in these coats,
and I expect the garments retained a certain characteristic
odour, so they apparently decided that the coats were a sort of
skin that we discarded. They clung to the empty sleeves, the
lapels, and the tails as though they had been glued on, and
while we went on with our work they would hang there, half
asleep, occasionally waking up to carry on a cackling conversation with us.

The great numbers of people who visited our campsite to
look round the collection always seemed most affected by our
group of baby monkeys. A baby monkey, in all its ways, is
very like a human baby, only infinitely more pathetic. The
women members of these parties would gaze at our young
monkeys with melting eyes, making inarticulate crooning
noises and brimming over with mother love. There was one
young lady who was so affected by the pathetic expressions
of the young monkeys that she rather unwisely took it upon
herself to deliver a lecture to me regarding the extreme cruelty
of taking these poor little creatures from their mothers and
incarcerating them in cages. She waxed quite poetical on the
joys of freedom and contrasted the carefree, happy existence
these babies would have had in the treetops with the ghastly
imprisonment for which I was responsible. That morning a
baby monkey had been brought in by a native hunter, and
since the young lady seemed to be such an expert on monkey
life in the treetops I suggested that she might like to help me
perform a little task that had to be gone through with each new
monkey that arrived. She agreed eagerly, seeing herself in the

role of a sort of a Florence Nightingale to simians. The little task consisted, quite simply, in searching the new baby for internal and external parasites. I explained this, and the young lady looked surprised; she said she didn't know monkeys had parasites—beyond fleas, of course. I produced the little basket the monkey was brought in, spread some of its excreta on a clean piece of paper, and showed her the numbers of thread-like worms it contained. My helper remained strangely silent.

Then I brought out the baby: he was a putty-nose guenon, an adorable little fellow clad in black fur with a white shirt-front and a gleaming, heart-shaped patch of white fur on his nose. I examined his tiny hands and feet, his long slender fingers and toes, and found no less than six jiggers comfortably ensconced. These minute creatures burrow their way into the skin of the feet and hands, particularly under the nails where the skin is soft, and there they eat and swell and grow until they reach the size of a match head. Then they lay their eggs and die. In due course the eggs hatch and the baby jiggers continue the good work that their parent had begun. If a jigger infection is not dealt with in the early stages it can lead to the loss of the joint of a toe or finger, and in extreme cases, all the toes or fingers, for the jiggers go on burrowing and breeding until they have hollowed the part out to a bag of skin filled with puss. I have had jiggers in my foot on several occasions and can vouch for the fact that they can be extremely painful. All this I explained to my helper in graphic detail. Then I got the tube of local anaesthetic, froze the fingers and toes of the little guenon, and with a sterilized needle proceeded to remove the jiggers and disinfect the wounds. I found this local anaesthetic a boon, for the operation is painful and the baby monkeys would not sit still otherwise.

When this was over I ran my fingers down the monkey's tail and felt two sausage-shaped swellings each as long as the first joint of my little finger and about the same circumference. I showed these to my companion and then parted the hair so that she could see the circular, porthole-like opening at the end of each swelling. Looking through into the interior of the swelling, you could see something white and loathsome moving. I explained, with my best Harley Street air, that a certain forest fly lays its eggs on the fur of various animals, and when the maggot hatches it burrows down into the flesh of its host and lives there, fattening like a pig in a sty, getting air through the porthole, and, when it finally leaves to turn into a fly, the host has a hole the circumference of a cigarette in its flesh, which generally becomes a suppurating sore. I showed my helper, who was by now quite pale, that it was impossible to hook these maggots out. I got the needle and, parting the hair, showed her the creature lying in its burrow like a miniature barrage balloon. As soon as the tip of the needle touched it, however, it compressed itself into a wrinkled blob, folding up like a concertina, and slid back into the depths of the monkey's tail. Then I showed her how to get them out, a method I had invented: pushing the nozzle of the anaesthetic tube into the porthole, I squirted the liquid inside until I had frozen the maggot into immobility; then, with a scalpel, I enlarged the porthole slightly, stabbed the maggot with the end of the needle, and withdrew it from its lair. As I pulled the horrible, wrinkled white horror out of the bloodstained hole my helper

left me precipitously. I removed the second maggot, disinfected
the gaping holes, and joined her at the other side of the camp
clearing. She explained that she was late for a lunch date,
thanked me for a most interesting morning, and took her leave,
never to visit us again. I always think it rather a pity that people
don't learn more about the drawbacks of life in the jungle
before prating about the cruelty of captivity.

One of the most delightful monkeys we had was a baby
moustached guenon, whom Smith procured on a trip up
country. He was the smallest monkey I had ever seen, and,
except for his long slender tail, he could fit comfortably into
a teacup. He was a greenish-grey in colour, with buttercup-
yellow cheek patches and a white shirtfront. But the most
incredible thing about him was his face, for across his upper
lip was a broad, curving band of white hair that made him look
as though he had an impressive moustache. For his size his
mouth was enormous, and so it could quite easily accommodate
the nipple of the feeding bottle. It was a most amusing sight to
see him hurl himself on the bottle, uttering shrill squeaks of
joy, wrap his arms and legs round it tightly, and lie there with
his eyes closed, sucking away frantically. It looked rather as
though he were being suckled by a large white airship, for the
bottle was three times his size. He was very quick to learn,
and it was not long before we had taught him to drink his milk
out of a saucer. He would be put on the camp table to be fed,
and as soon as he saw the saucer approaching he would get quite
hysterical with excitement, trembling and twitching and
screaming at the top of his voice. As soon as the saucer was
placed before him he would, without any hesitation, dive head
first into it. He would push his face completely under the milk

BABY MOUSTACHED GUENON

and come up for air only when he could hold out no longer. Sometimes, in his greed, he would wait too long, and a shower of bubbles would break the surface, and he would follow them, coughing and sneezing and spattering himself and the table with a fountain of milk. There were times during his meal when he would be convinced that you were hanging around waiting for an opportunity to take his saucer away, and, giving a quavering scream of rage, he would frustate your plan by the simple expedient of leaping into the air and landing in the centre of the saucer with a splash, where he would sit, glaring at you triumphantly. At mealtimes he would get his head and face so covered with milk that it was difficult to tell where his moustache began and ended, and the table looked as though someone had milked a large healthy cow over it.

The two most forceful characters in our monkey collection were, of course, the chimpanzees, Mary and Charlie. Charlie had been the pet of a planter before he came to us, and he was fairly well domesticated. He had a small, wrinkled, sorrowful face and melting brown eyes; he looked as though the world had treated him harshly but that he was too much of a saint to complain. This wounded, dejected air was a lot of moonshine, for Charlie, far from being an ill-treated, misunderstood ape, was a disgraceful little street urchin, full of low cunning and deceit. Every day we used to let him out of his cage for exercise, and he would roam about the camp, looking radiantly innocent, until he thought he had lulled you into believing in his integrity. Then he would wander nonchalantly towards the food table, give a quick glance round to see if he was observed, grab the largest bunch of bananas within reach, and dash madly away towards the nearest tree. If you gave chase he would drop the fruit and skid to a standstill. Then he would sit in the dust while you scolded him, gazing up at you sorrowfully, the picture of injured innocence, the expression on his face showing quite plainly that he was being wrongfully accused of a monstrous crime but that he was far too noble to point that out to you if you were too obtuse to realize it. Wave the bunch of stolen fruit under his nose and he would regard it with faint surprise, mingled with disgust. Why should you imagine that I stole the fruit? his expression seemed to say. Are you not aware of the fact that I dislike bananas? Never in my whole life (devoted to philanthropy and self-denial) have I felt the slightest inclination even to sample the loathsome fruit, much less steal any. The scolding over, Charlie would rise, give a deep sigh, throw you a look of compassion tinged with disgust, and lope off to the kitchen to see what he could steal there. He was quite incorrigible, and his face was so expressive that he could carry on a long conversation without any need of speech.

Charlie's greatest triumph came when we received a visit from the High Commissioner for the Cameroons, who was passing through on one of his periodical visits of inspection.

CHARLIE, THE CHIMPANZEE

He came down to our camp, accompanied by a vast army of secretaries and other supporters. He was greatly interested in our large array of beasts, but Charlie attracted him most. While we explained what a hypocrite the ape was, Charlie was holding the great man's hand through the bars of his cage and gazing up at him with woebegone expression and pleading eyes, begging His Excellency not to listen to the foul slander we were uttering. When His Excellency left he invited Smith and myself to his At Home, which was to take place the following evening.

The next morning a most impressive messenger, glittering with golden buttons, delivered an envelope from the District Office. Inside was a large card informing us, in magnificent twirly writing, that His Excellency, High Commissioner for the Cameroons, requested the pleasure of Charlie's presence during his At Home, between the hours of six and eight. When we showed it to Charlie he was sitting in his cage meditating; he gave it a brief glance, then ignored it. His attitude told us he was quite used to being showered with such invitations, but that these were too worldly to be of any interest to him. He was, he implied, far too busy with his saintlike meditations to get excited about invitations to drinking orgies with mere High Commissioners. As he had been into the kitchen that morning and stolen six eggs, a loaf of bread, and a leg of cold chicken we did not believe him.

Mary was a chimp of completely different character. She was older than Charlie, and much bigger, being about the size of a two-year-old human. Before we bought her she had been in the hands of a Hausa trader, and, I am afraid, she must have been teased and ill treated, for at first she was sullen and vicious, and we feared we would never be able to gain her confidence, as she had developed a deep-rooted mistrust of anything human, black or white. But after a few months of good food and kind handling she delighted us by blossoming forth into a chimp with much charm, a sunny disposition, and a terrific sense of humour. She had a pale pink, rather oafish face and a large potbelly. She reminded me of a fat barmaid ready to laugh uproariously at some bawdy jest. After she got to know and trust us she developed a trick she thought was frightfully funny. She would lie back in her cage, balanced precariously on her perch, and present an unmentionable part of her anatomy to the bars. You were then expected to lean forward and blow hard, whereupon Mary would utter a screech of laughter and modestly cover herself with her hands. Then she would give you a coy look from over the mound of her stomach and uncover herself again, and you were expected to repeat this mirth-provoking action. This became known in camp as Blowing Mary's Wicked Parts, and no matter how many times a day you repeated it, Mary still found it exceedingly funny. She would throw back her head and open her mouth wide, showing vast areas of pink gum and white teeth, hooting and tittering with hysterical laughter.

Although Mary treated us and the staff with great gentleness, she never forgot that she had a grudge against Africans in general, and she used to pick on any strange ones that came to camp, to get her own back. She would grin at them ingratiatingly and slap her chest or turn somersaults—anything to gain their attention. By her antics she would lure them closer and closer to the cage, looking the picture of cheerful good humour, while her shrewd eyes judged the distance carefully.

Suddenly the long, powerful arm would shoot out through the bars, there would be a loud ripping noise, a yelp of fright from the African, and Mary would dance round her cage, triumphantly waving a torn shirt or singlet that she had pulled off her admirer's back. Her strength was extraordinary, and it cost me a small fortune in replacements, until I put her cage in such a position that she could not commit these outrages.

The monkey collection kept up a continuous noise all through the day, but in the afternoon, about four-thirty, this rose to a crescendo of sound that would tax the hardest nerves, for it was at this time that the monkeys had their milk. About four they would start to get impatient, leaping and jumping about their cages, turning somersaults or sitting with their faces pressed to the bars, squeaking mournfully. As soon as the line of clean pots was laid out and the great kerosene tin—full of warm milk, malt, cod-liver oil, sugar, and calcium—came in sight, a wave of excitement would sweep the cages and the uproar would be deafening. The chimps would give prolonged hoots through pursed lips and thump on the sides of their cages with their fists; the drills would utter their penetrating "ar-ar-ar-ar-ar-erererer!" cries, like miniature machine guns; the guenons would give faint birdlike whistles and trills; the patas monkeys would dance up and down like mad ballerinas, shouting "proup, proup" plaintively; and the beautiful Colobus, with her swaying shawl of white and black hair, would call "arroup! arroup! arroup! ye-ye-ye-ye!" in a commanding tone of voice. As we moved along the cages, pushing the pots of milk through the doors, the noises would gradually cease, until all that could be heard was a low snoring, sucking sound, interspersed with an occasional cough as some milk went down the wrong way.

Then, the pots empty, the monkeys would climb up on their perches and sit there, their bellies bulging, uttering loud, satisfied belches at regular intervals. After a while they would all climb down to the floor to examine their pots and make quite sure there was no milk left, even picking them up and looking underneath. Then they would curl up on their perches in the evening sun and fall into a bloated stupor, while peace came to the camp.

One of the things I find particularly endearing about monkeys is their lack of inhibition. They will perform any action they feel like with no embarrassment. They will urinate copiously, or bend down and watch their own faeces appear with expressions of absorbed interest; they will mate or masturbate with great freedom regardless of any audience. I have heard embarrassed human beings call monkeys dirty, filthy creatures when they have watched them innocently perform these actions in public, and it is an attitude of mind that I always find difficult to understand. After all, it is we, with our superior intelligence, who have decided that the perfectly natural functions of our bodies are something unclean. Monkeys do not share our view.

The Africans also have this innocent attitude towards the functions of the body. I had a wonderful example of this one day when a couple of rather stuffy missionaries came to look round the camp.

I showed them our various animals and birds, and they made a lot of unctuous comments about them. Then we came to the monkeys, and the missionaries were delighted with them. Presently, however, we reached a cage where a monkey was sitting on the perch in a curious hunched-up attitude.

"Oh! What's *he* doing?" cried the lady gaily, and before I could prevent her she had bent down to get a better look. She shot up again, her face a deep, rich scarlet, for the monkey had been whiling away the hours to milk time by sitting there and sucking himself.

We hurried through the rest of the monkey collection in record time, and I was much amused by the expression of frozen disgust that had replaced the look of benevolent delight on the lady missionary's face. They might be God's creatures, her expression implied, but she wished He would do something about their habits. As we rounded the corner of the marquee we were greeted by another of God's creatures in the shape of a lanky African hunter. He was a man who had brought in specimens regularly each week, but for the past fortnight he had not come near us.

"Iseeya, Samuel," I greeted him.

"Iseeya, Masa," he said, coming towards us.

"Which side you done go all dis time?" I asked. "Why you never bring me beef for two weeks, eh?"

"Eh! Masa, I done get sickness."

"Sickness? Eh, sorry, my friend. Na what sickness you get?"

"Na my gonorrhea, Masa," he explained. "My gonorrhea de worry me too much."

The missionaries were among the people who never called twice.

IN WHICH WE WALKA GOOD

The last few days before joining the ship that is to take you
back to England are always the most hectic of the whole trip.
There are a thousand things that have to be done: lorries to
hire, cages to strengthen, vast quantities of food to be purchased and crated up, and all this on top of the normal routine
work of maintaining the collection.

One of the things that worried us most were the *Idiurus*.
Our colony had by now diminished to four specimens, and we
were determined to get these safely back to England. We had,
after superhuman efforts, got them to eat avocado pears as well
as palm nuts, and on this they seemed to do quite well. I decided that if we took three dozen avocados with us, in varying
stages from ripe to green, there would be enough to last the

voyage with some left over to use in England while the *Idiurus* were settling down. Accordingly, I called Jacob and informed him that he must procure three dozen avocados without delay. To my surprise, he looked at me as though I had taken leave of my senses.

"Avocado pear, sah?" he asked.

"Yes, avocado pear," I said.

"I no fit get um, sah," he said mournfully.

"You no fit get um? Why not?"

"Avocado pear done finish," said Jacob helplessly.

"Finish? What you mean, finish? I want you go for market and get um, not from kitchen."

"Done finish for market, sah," said Jacob patiently.

What he was trying to explain suddenly dawned on me: the season for avocado pears had finished, and he could not get me any. I would have to face the voyage with no supply of the fruit for the precious *Idiurus*.

It was just like the *Idiurus*, I reflected bitterly, to start eating something when it was going out of season. However, avocados I had to have, and so in the few days at our disposal I marshalled the staff and made them scour the countryside for the fruit. By the time we were ready to move down country we had obtained twelve small shrivelled avocados, and that was all. These almost mummified remains had to last until we reached England.

We had to travel some two hundred miles down to the coast from our base camp, and it required three lorries and a small van to carry our collection. We travelled by night, for it was cooler for the animals, and the journey took us two days. It was, quite frankly, one of the worst journeys I can remember.

We had to stop the lorries every three hours, take out all the
frog boxes, and sprinkle them with cold water to prevent them
from drying up. Twice during each night we had to make
prolonged stops to bottle-feed the young animals on warm
milk, which we carried ready mixed in thermos flasks. Then,
when dawn came, we had to pull the lorries to the side of
the road, under the shade of the great trees, unload every
single cage onto the grass, and clean and feed every specimen.
On the morning of the third day we arrived at the small rest
house on the coast that had been put at our disposal; here everything had to be unpacked once again and cleaned and fed before we could crawl into the house, eat a meal, and collapse
on our beds to sleep.

That evening parties of people from the local banana plan-
tations came round to see the animals, and, half dead with sleep,
we were forced to conduct tours, answer questions, and be
polite.

"Are you travelling on this ship that's in?" inquired someone.

"Yes," I said, stifling a yawn. "Sailing tomorrow."

"Good Lord! I pity you then," he said cheerfully.

"Oh. Why is that?"

"Captain's a bloody Tartar, old boy, and he hates animals.
It's a fact. Old Robinson wanted to take his pet baboon back
with him on this ship when he went on leave last time. Captain
chucked it off. Wouldn't have it on board. Said he didn't want
his ship filled with stinking monkeys. Frightful uproar about it,
so I heard."

Smith and I exchanged anxious looks, for of all the evils
that can befall a collector an unsympathetic captain is perhaps

the worst. Later, when the last party of sightseers had gone, we discussed this disturbing bit of news. We decided that we should have to go out of our way to be polite to the captain; and we would take extra care to make sure there were no untoward incidents among the monkeys to earn his wrath.

Our collection was placed on the forward deck under the supervision of the chief officer, a charming, helpful man. The captain we did not see that night, and the next morning, when we arose early to clean out the cages, he was pacing the bridge, a hunched, terrifying figure. We had been told that he would be down to breakfast, and we were looking forward to meeting him with some trepidation.

"Remember," said Smith as we cleaned out the monkeys, "we must keep on the right side of him." He filled a basket full of sawdust, trotted to the rail, and cast it into the sea. "We must be careful not to do anything to annoy him," he went on when he had returned.

Just at that moment a figure in a spotless white uniform came running breathlessly down from the bridge. "Excuse me, sir," he said, "but the captain's compliments, sir, and will you please make sure which way the wind's blowing before you chuck that sawdust overboard."

Horror-stricken, we looked up towards the bridge: the air was full of swirling fragments of sawdust, and the captain, scowling angrily, was brushing his bespattered uniform.

"Please apologize to the captain for us," I said, conquering a frightful desire to laugh.

When the officer had gone I turned to Smith. "Keep on the right side of him," I said bitterly. "Don't do anything to annoy him. Only fling sawdust all over him and his precious bridge. Trust you to know the right way to a captain's heart."

When the gong sounded we hurried down to our cabin, washed, and took our seats in the dining saloon. We found, to our dismay, that we were seated at the captain's table. The captain sat with his back to the bulkhead, in which there were three portholes, and Smith and I sat on the opposite side of the circular table. The portholes looked out into the well deck in which our collection was stocked. Halfway through the meal the captain had thawed out a little and was even starting to make tolerant little jokes about sawdust.

"As long as you don't let anything escape, I don't mind," he said jovially, disembowelling a fried egg.

"Oh, we won't let that happen," I said, and the words were hardly out of my mouth when something moved in the port- hole, and, glancing up, I saw Sweeti-pie, the black-eared squir- rel, perched in the opening, examining the interior of the saloon with a kindly eye. The captain, of course, could not see the squirrel, sitting on a level with his shoulder and about three feet away, and he went on eating and talking unconcernedly, while behind him Sweeti-pie sat on his hind legs and cleaned his whiskers. For a few seconds I was so startled my brain refused to function, and I sat there gaping at the porthole. Luckily the captain was too intent on his breakfast to notice. Sweeti-pie finished his wash and brush-up and began to look round the saloon again. He decided that the place would be worth in- vestigating and glanced around to see which was the best way to get down from his perch. He decided that the quickest method would be to jump from the porthole onto the captain's shoulder. I could see this plan taking shape in the little brute's head, and the thought of his landing on the captain's shoulder galvanized me into action. Muttering a hasty "Excuse me," I pushed back my chair and walked out of the saloon. As soon as I was out of sight of the captain I ran as fast as I could out onto the deck. To my relief, Sweeti-pie had not jumped, and his long bushy tail was still hanging outside the porthole. I flung myself across the hatch cover and grabbed him by his tail just as he bunched himself up to spring. I bundled him, chattering indignantly, into his cage, and then returned, flushed but triumphant, to the saloon. The captain was still talking, and, if he had noticed my abrupt departure at all, he must have attributed it to the pangs of nature, for he made no mention of it.

On the third day of the voyage two of the *Idiurus* were dead. I was examining their corpses sorrowfully when a member of the crew appeared. He asked why the little animals had died, and I explained the tragic tale of the nonexistent avocado pears.

"What's an avocado pear?" he inquired.

I showed him one of the shrivelled wrecks.

"Oh, those things," he said. "Do you want some?"

I gazed at him speechlessly for a minute. "Have you got some?" I said at last.

"Well," he said, "I haven't exactly got any, but I think I can get you some."

That evening he reappeared with his pockets bulging. "Here," he said, stuffing some beautifully ripe avocados into my hand, "give me three of yours, and don't say a word to anyone."

I gave him three of my dried-up fruits and hastily fed the

Idiurus with the ripe ones he had procured, and they enjoyed them thoroughly. My spirits rose, and I began to have hopes once more of landing them in England. My sailor friend brought me plump, ripe avocados whenever I informed him that my stock was running low, and he always took some of my desiccated stock in exchange. It was very curious, but I felt the best thing I could do was not to inquire too deeply into the matter.

In spite of the fresh fruit, another *Idiurus* died, and by the time we were rolling through the Bay of Biscay I had precisely one specimen left. It was now, I realized, a fight against time: if I could keep this solitary specimen alive until we reached England I would have a tremendous variety of food to offer it, and I felt sure that I could find something it would eat. As we drew closer and closer to England I watched the little chap carefully. He seemed fit and in the best of spirits. As an additional precaution, I smuggled his cage into my cabin each night, so that he would not catch a chill. The day before we docked he was in fine fettle, and I became almost convinced that I would land him. That night, quite suddenly and for no apparent reason, he died. So, after travelling four thousand miles, the last *Idiurus* died twenty-four hours out of Liverpool. I was bitterly disappointed, and black depression settled on me.

The hairy frogs had come through, as had the brow-leaf toads. Charlie and Mary were hooting in their cages as they were swung overboard. Sweeti-pie was eating a sugar lump and eyeing the crowd on the docks with hopeful eyes, while the moustached monkey peered from his cage, his whiskers gleaming, looking like a juvenile Santa Claus. But even the sight of all

these creatures being landed safely after so long and so dangerous a trip did not altogether compensate me for the loss of my
little *Idiurus*.

Smith and I were just going to leave the ship when my sailor
friend appeared. He had heard the news and was extremely upset to think that our combined efforts had been in vain.

"By the way," I said, "I'm very curious to know where you
got those avocado pears from in midocean."

He glanced round to make sure we were not overheard. "I'll
tell you, mate, only keep it under your hat," he said in a hoarse
whisper. "The captain's very partial to an avocado, see, and
he has a big box of them in the fridge. He always brings home
a box, see? I just got some of them for you."

"Do you mean to say those were the captain's avocados?" I
asked faintly.

"Sure. But he won't miss 'em," my friend assured me cheerfully. "You see, every time I took some of his out I put the
same number of yours back in the box."

The customs men could not understand why I kept shaking
with laughter as I was showing them our crates, and they kept
darting suspicious looks at me. But it was not, unfortunately,
the sort of joke you could share.